Beauty Exposed
Captivating Stories of Life with Siblings who have Down Syndrome

By: Chloe Goulding

DEDICATION

I want to dedicate this book to my two siblings who have Down syndrome; Charity and Neko you have both taught me so much and I love you to pieces!!!

What People are Saying About Beauty Exposed

"Beauty Exposed" is a wonderfully written, candid account of people interacting with siblings with Down syndrome. I thoroughly enjoyed reading the collection of stories that portrayed life with Down syndrome. As a mother of multiple children, including a daughter with Down syndrome, it is encouraging to see that while life may have been more challenging at times, all of the stories are filled with love for their siblings. As a sibling of a brother with many special needs, it was surprising how accurate and similar the stories were to some I could tell. Growing up with a family member with special needs is challenging. I especially enjoyed the stories that included the hard times, like the child who was sometimes afraid of her sister hurting her or the siblings with tantrums because of frustration and language delays. Stories that include the challenges and heartaches of real life help to validate the book's authenticity. Reading the stories of adult siblings was especially heartwarming, since this is my daily life with my brother. I have fond memories of our childhood and the life lessons that I learned that simply cannot be taught without experience. "Beauty Exposed" carefully catches the feelings of siblings both young and old and tells a complete story of growing up with a sibling with Down syndrome.

Courtney Ziegler – Adoptive mother to a child with Down syndrome

The Angels on Stage family and I congratulate Chloe Goulding on her first book! I was touched as I read each story and found myself engrossed in the intimate details of each unique relationship. As I continued to read the stories, I felt this deep connection to the siblings and their experiences as well as the amazing individuals with Down syndrome who made such a lasting impact in the lives of so many. I found myself in tears of joy and heartbreak as I read the truly personal and heartfelt stories that were shared. It's like taking a trip down memory road as each sibling shares life through their lens and talked about the friendships, love, and ups and downs of having a sibling with Down syndrome. Intimate, entertaining, and touching...are just some of the words that come to mind in this collection of stories which pull at your heartstrings. Thank you for helping others understand a little more deeply, by letting the reader enter a small part of the world of siblings of those with Down syndrome. These stories give us a glimpse that people with Down syndrome have a lot to offer their families and the world. I hope all the readers will see that and start to believe that too. It reminds me of what we say at Angels on Stage, "....*and when all those people believe in you, deep enough and strong enough believe in you...it stands to reason that you yourself will start to see what everybody sees in you*". *Bravo, Chloe, for getting people to believe in all the amazing young people and adults with Down syndrome - you are changing perceptions and raising awareness in sharing these brave and loving siblings' stories.*

Nina Duncan - VP Programs of Angels on Stage

~~~~~~

In her debut book, Chloe shares candid, personal stories from those who have siblings with Down syndrome. In doing so, she encourages readers to see that in the fabric of our lives, siblings with Down syndrome are weaving both burlap and gold thread. Their presence in our families brings the rough texture and strength of burlap, intricately woven with the beauty and value of gold thread. Both fabrics are necessary, both have meaning.

Katie Carper – Adoptive mother to a child with Down syndrome

~~~~~~

Chloe Goulding does a great job her first time out as an author. Beauty Exposed takes us into the lives of siblings of individuals with Down syndrome. In sharing their story, the siblings are opening their heart and home to the reader, and showing us the true meaning of family. I hope this book is the first of many for Chloe!

Stephanie – Director of NDSAN

~~~~~~

While I immediately loved the premise of this book, I am even more excited about getting it into libraries and school everywhere... and soon! You are so right that children with Down syndrome "are" a blessing in so many ways and shame on us for singling them out for in vitro testing! The world sure would be happier and more joyful if there were more children like these in each community.

Olenka Villarreal – Founder of the Magical Bridge Park in Palo Alto

Each story was written from the heart and many I could relate to as a mother of a child with Down syndrome. They were funny, honest and a great perspective from a siblings point of view

Teresa Fujishin-Gruber, M.A. – 321life CEO and mother to a child with Down syndrome

CONTENTS

FOREWORD

Chloe Goulding came into my life almost 6 years ago. When she was around age 10. We met because my grandson Neko James, who has Down syndrome was being put up for adoption, and Chloe's family had offered to adopt Neko. Chloe's family had previously adopted another baby, Charity Rose, with Down syndrome, and I was really surprised to learn that they were willing to adopt another child with Down syndrome because Charity Rose, had had so many problems, even going into cardiac arrest at age 3. You would think after everything that family went through with Charity Rose that one adopted child with Down syndrome would be more than enough, but they prayed about it, and the Lord set them on the path of adopting Neko. That open adoption has blessed me with my biological grandson Neko plus five adopted grandchildren that I love and adore equally! My family and friends, along with Neko's biological parents, are all involved with the Goulding family, and everyone is sharing in the joy of this most amazing adoption.

One of the first things that impressed me about Chloe was that she was helping her mother with home school duties for Charity and her other four biological siblings. She seemed very relaxed and patient with her adopted sister Charity, who was four years old at the time. Not that her other siblings weren't aware of Charity, but Chloe at her tender age had made it a point to really be there and know what her little sister's wants and needs were, and you could tell in an instant that Charity was crazy in love with Chloe!

Chloe has seen and done more than most adults when it comes to Down syndrome. She has made it a big part of her life and has worked with Charity and the Angels on Stage company, which puts on theater shows for kids with all sorts of disabilities. She has been Charity's buddy for 3 or 4 years with Angels on Stage, and you can tell even when Charity is not feeling her best, Chloe still shows her little sister all the love she can give. Sometimes assisting in the care of a child with Down syndrome can be very trying for an adult, let alone a young girl. Now at the age of 16 Chloe has mastered the art quite beautifully! Chloe and her siblings have also raised a lot of money by holding rallies and walks for Angels on Stage and Real Options, which is a pro-life clinic for parents, unwed parents, and teenagers who are considering abortion! If you've ever driven past Real Options in San Jose, California, you might have seen Chloe and her older brother Tucker outside the clinic, silently praying for those mothers or mothers to be to choose life for their babies when entering Real Options. She knows in her heart that Real Options will do its very best to save the unborn child while still caring about the mother to be.

When Chloe was just 14, she decided that she wanted to put out a book about Down syndrome and began questioning her parents about the condition. Her unconditional love for both Charity and Neko is heartfelt, and she wanted to share their stories with the world. With the love and guidance of her parents and their many prayers, her book began to come into existence.

Chloe decided that telling her stories about Charity and Neko would be beautiful (hence, the title, *Beauty Exposed*), and so she asked, "Why not share the stories of other siblings that have a brother or sister with Down syndrome?" That put her on a path to hearing and collecting the many different stories other siblings had written and which are included in Chloe's book. Some of the stories will touch your heart and bring tears to your eyes while others will make you joyously laugh.

Now at 16, Chloe's expertise on the matter of Down

syndrome has her wondering how she can give back to those who work so diligently at saving and working with those with Down syndrome. Her book is genuine, heartfelt, and a wonderful look in the eyes of those with Down syndrome! Chloe has always said that the eyes of those with Down syndrome are the shapes of the rainbows. Now isn't that just beautiful? I hope you enjoy Chloe's book as much as I do!!

I would now like to share with you my very first visit with my grandson Neko and his new and amazing family and now my darling adopted family!!!

The following is a letter I wrote to my friends and family, including Neko's new family, to tell them about my first visit to the Gouldings.

When I read this sentence in a book, "We need to take time to embrace the person who's struggling," I thought of all of you!!!! I wanted to write during this particular Holiday because I wanted each of you to know how thankful I am to have you in my life. Thank you for your prayers, hugs, thoughts and even your tears, your kindness, gentleness and faithfulness has really touched my heart. You all are very near and dear to me and I hope to be there for you if ever you're in need. I wanted to share with you my first visit to Neko James and his New Family.

The day I first met Neko's new mom Elizabeth Goulding, I found her to be kind, gentle and soft spoken and just as emotional as we were about the adoption, but I didn't quite realize yet just how special she and her family really are. From the beginning they have invited us to be part of Neko's life. We call and email each other and continue to share our lives. When I was invited to see Neko and meet his new family, I was overjoyed. On this past Saturday I took the 2-1/2 hour drive to their home in San Jose. I was a little nervous as I stepped out of my car. That soon passed as the majority of the family came running out to me calling out, "Grandma D, Grandma D, we're so happy you're here." I received hugs from everyone, and Elizabeth touched my arm and tilted her head toward the front door, stating that Ellie wanted to be the presenter of Neko. There, in the doorway was this petite but beautiful little girl with short blonde hair and the cutest little bangs. She was holding Neko and waiting for me to step forward. As I approached her, she held up Neko and said, "Here Grandma D; here's your baby Grandson Neko." At that very moment I felt the breath of God fill my body, the rush of love fill my soul, and the pains of 2009 [a death in my family] wash away. This was a blessing that I had been praying and hoping for, and it finally arrived. The Goulding family were also a blessing for my son Justin and Mary, which they will realize and understand more clearly later.

I spent the day there holding and feeding Neko and massaging his foot that was turned a bit from being cramped up while in the womb, and I got that little smile I always got when I did that. Harrison, who is four, would come up to us and kiss Neko on the cheek and say, "Your Grandma D is holding you, Neko." I brought crafts that Tucker, Chloe, Ellie and I did while Harrison and Charity took naps and MaMa Elizabeth baked cookies. Pa Pa Will, I'm sure, is the true Mr. Mom in their lives and is just as sweet as the rest of them.

All in all it was a wonderful day and when I left, I was filled to the brim with joy and happiness, and I am still floating. I will be seeing them again around Christmas, and I can't wait to see them all and hug, kiss and smell all over Neko.

This family is truly loved by the Lord, and they have love, joy, peace, patience, kindness, goodness, gentleness, faithfulness and self-control wrapped all around them, and we are blessed to know them and be a part of their lives. Happy Holidays to you all.

Love, Grandma D, Auntie, Debbie Do and Mom! xoxo

My life, Their life, Our life

Written by: Chloe Goulding

One ordinary day, an ordinary family was sitting on an ordinary couch, in an ordinary house, and well, you get the picture. This family was reading the Bible together and praying. Shortly after, the phone rang. The children could tell it was an important phone call and remained quiet as their mother spoke on the phone. They got the feeling that it might be a phone call about a baby, so, the little girls prayed for a sister and convinced their brother to do the same. God answered their prayers; and He answered with a yes! The following day, the four children, along with their mother, drove an hour in order to meet their new little sister. She was abandoned, without a loving family, and without a name. She had midnight black hair, a cute little button nose, and chubby cheeks. She was perfect! After the children and mother got to say "hello", it was time to head home. The next day they were able to visit again, this time though, an ambulance team arrived to take this new little baby to a more advanced hospital in San Francisco. After about a week, the family was finally able to bring their baby home.

For the next few years, life was busy and exhausting for the mother who not only cared for her little newborn daughter, but also a 7 month old son. The growing family chose to name their baby girl Charity Rose; Charity means love.

~~~~~~

This is my family; Charity is my sister. This is about my life; it's about their life; it's our life.

~~~~~~

A lot of the people we knew thought my parents were crazy for adopting a newborn with Down syndrome while they already had four other children, not to mention that the youngest was only seven months old! Yes, my parents might have seemed a little crazy, but they were just following God who was in the lead. God adopted each of us into his family, so why should we not extend the same offer?

Life was very busy when Charity came home. Being the oldest girl, I had lots of opportunities to help Mom take care of the babies, which of course I loved! I remember rocking Harrison to sleep in the big rocking chair and then laying him down to sleep in the bassinet. Our homeschool studies that year may have been more about how to feed, burp, dress, and bathe babies than about math and English. During that time in our lives, Charity was in and out of the hospital with different health problems. She had pneumonia three times, which resulted in a several stays at Good Samaritan Hospital. Once we even had to call 911, but that's a story in itself. Charity had always been a fussy baby, but we assumed it was part of who she was. Right around her 3rd birthday, she was particularly grumpy and fussy. On the night of March 29th, Charity fussed throughout the night, so Mom held and cuddled her later telling me she had felt that this would be the last time she held Charity for a very long time. The next day we took Charity to the hospital to have blood work done, since something was obviously wrong. Grandma Alice and Grandpa Henry came to stay with us that night to help our family. I remember lying in my bed that night, when suddenly the phone started ringing. Mom started leaving a message with a shaky voice, "Charity just went into cardiac arrest. They resuscitated her but it is bad." Of course, since I was only 10 years old, I really didn't know what cardiac arrest meant, but from the tone and sound of her voice, I knew it must be really bad!

When mom and dad came home from the hospital the next morning, they repeated what the doctor had told them, "There is nothing more we can do for Charity." We spent time praying and crying together asking God to spare our little Charity. That very same morning, the Doctor called to tell us there was one more possibility – transporting Charity to Lucile Packard Children's Hospital in Palo Alto, CA to use the ECMO machine. A few hours later the transport team was ready, but needed Mom and Dad's consent on paper. Dad and Mom arrived at the hospital, only to find out that Good Samaritan was having a fire drill, complete with the firefighters. Since this was the case, they could not use the elevators. On the way to finding the stairs, they encountered another problem. Two very overly helpful women at the volunteer counter were not going to let Mom and Dad go up those stairs. My parents knew that quite possibly Charity's life depended on them getting up there. They both tried reasoning with the women, but to no avail. Finally, they figured their only hope was to be a little sneaky and get to the staircase. Eventually they made it to Charity's room, where they met her transportation team. The team made sure my parents understood how critical Charity was and that she might not make it to the hospital.

~~~~~~

My mom and dad said they had us go outside and wave goodbye to Charity in case she did not make it.

~~~~~~

When the ambulance arrived at Lucile Packard, Charity was still alive. After stabilizing her, the 3 month long stay at Lucile Packard began. In those three months she had many surgeries; too many for me to count, which included open heart surgery, inserting a g-tube, ballooning her trachea and putting her on the ECMO machine. During that time, my parents both felt that God was leading them to adopt another baby with Down syndrome. Charity had been home nearly five months when my mom flew down to San Diego to pick up the newest addition to our family – Neko James Goulding. We were beyond thrilled!!! There was only one little problem; around that same time I developed a rash on my face and arm, so a day or so after Neko came home, my grandparents took me to the Doctor's office. The doctor didn't think it was anything bad, but just in case she prescribed me an antibiotic, and gave strict orders not to hold my newest little brother for an agonizing 4 DAYS!!! As you can probably imagine, that was one of the worst punishments anyone could have given me as a 10 year old who loved her new little brother. I was so relieved when the days of agony were over and I could once again resume my post as mom's right hand girl.

My two siblings – Charity and Neko – have taught me so much about many things; I'd like to share some of them with you..... First of all, they've shown me how important it is to enjoy the small things in life: the things that we overlook too often. Sometimes we all (me included) tend to get wrapped up in planning ahead and thinking about what is coming up next, and while that's okay sometimes, most of the time we should be living in the moment and enjoying small things like pushing a little one in the swing, reading a great book out in the sunshine, washing all those dishes while being thankful that there's that many people in the house to make those dishes dirty, running, etc....

Another lesson my siblings have taught me is how to look at/treat people for who they are and not for what they might look like at the outside. For example, we live right by a high school, and so everyday around 2:30pm a lot of the teens walk down our street to get home. Sometimes we're outside when this happens and Charity will go up to a random person that walks by and she'll give them a hug. The student will usually respond with a hug, smile, and a "Hi - thanks for the hug!" Then, they will walk away with a huge smile on their face! It's like Charity knows who needs a little extra love and she won't be afraid to deliver it. Sometimes I see someone who looks, acts, dresses, or talks differently, and it can be kind of scary at times to be available to be a friend to that person. I've just started to know what it feels like to have that peer pressure and not want to be "the weird one" for talking to someone who is unique. It's very hard, but my siblings are a great reminder not to let the fear of not being "cool" get in the way. When school is hard or the going gets rough, Charity and Neko have taught me to not give up. In our house we're not allowed to say "I can't" or "It's too hard." People with Down syndrome have to work like 10x harder than we do to do things like walk, ride a bike, or talk. So when things are hard, it's not the time to give up; it's the perfect time to give it your all! One day during my Fashion Design and Textile Art class, we were having our break time. Some of the kids started talking about the "Special Ed kids" at their schools. This was the first time that my mom wasn't there to give them a lesson in "not making fun of my child who has Down syndrome," and it was the first time it was my peers talking about this and a time I would need to stand up for my siblings. Instantly, my ears were alert for any signs of making fun of my siblings - or other kids with special needs. I listened very intently to the whole conversation, but to my great relief, they poked no fun all them at all. Instead they talked about how well they could dance, how smart they were, and how accepting their schools were of these kids!

Soon after I started my Fashion Design & Textile Art class we had a "Back to School" night for the families to come and see what their student had been working on and what things they would be learning in the months to follow. I was watching Charity so my parents could look around, and at that time Charity had really been into dropping spit balls wherever she was. At that moment she decided to spit on the floor in my classroom. I told her "no, we don't spit" and then happened to look up – my teacher was standing there and I'm assuming she saw the whole thing. It was Charity's way of introducing herself. Another time, as I was getting ready to climb into bed, I saw a dark shadow and assuming it was my pillow I got in and tried to get comfortable. Except, it wasn't my pillow, it was my sweet Charity, waiting for me to come to bed.

After having Charity and Neko in my life, I believe that everyone should have someone with Down syndrome in their life and I find myself feeling badly for those who don't. Rather than seeing their disabilities, I see their possibilities and wish that everyone could see what I see. **The beauty is there, waiting to be exposed.**

Beauty Exposed

A NOTE TO PARENTS EXPECTING A BABY WITH DOWN SYNDROME:

First of all I want to extend my warmest congratulations to you and your family about the little one on their way! I want you to know that from a sibling's perspective a person with Down syndrome is one of the best presents you could ever give to your child! People with Down syndrome teach us things that no one else can teach – they are some of the best examples of God's unfailing love. I'm praying that this book and these stories show what a wonderful gift people with Down syndrome are and how they enrich our lives every single day!!!

~Chloe Goulding

Beauty Exposed

Stories Written by School Age Siblings

These stories are written by siblings between the ages of 4 & 13 years old. These children share from their hearts what it means to have a sibling with Down syndrome in a fun and humorous way!

Beauty Exposed

My Best Friend

Written by: James Leach

My best friend is my sister. She is my best friend because she is kind. And because she is thotthule (thoughtful). And because she helps me when im (I'm) hert (hurt). She is a good friend when she plays puppy with me. (a game they play). And also when i'm hunngre (hungry) she gives me a snack.

My Brother Charlie

Written by: Calvin Robinson

Hi. My name is Calvin. I'm five-and-a-half years old. My brother has Down syndrome. He always tackles me because he is very strong. He is stronger than me, because he is seven-and-a-half. My brother is very funny. I like that he goes to my school. He has more chromosomes than me, because the egg might have had an extra one. He was born at a hospital, and his name is Charlie. I like my brother Charlie.

Sheer Joy

Written by: Reata Lucore

I know you want to know about Levi. First, my mom saw that she was pregnant.

Well, when my mom had Levi, she was a little sad because he had Down syndrome.

When we got x-rays, he was already cute! But I was scared too! But he became a sheer joy!

I loved Levi the minute I saw him. He was so cute!

If you had him I would visit him every day. If we had another Levi, oh that would be so nice!

Reata and Levi on their ranch!

Author's Note - We met Reata's family before her mom had given birth to Levi. They asked our family if we'd be willing to adopt Levi – and we said yes! When he was born though, his family fell in love with him and decided to keep him for themselves and we are so thankful they did! ~Chloe

The Sweetness in His Heart

Written by: Dawson Fitzgerald

My name is Dawson Fitzgerald. I am the second of 4 kids. Jake is 13, I am 11, Garrett is 10 and Carly is 6. Garrett was born with Down syndrome.

Garrett is the most fun, sweetest, cutest guy I know. He is always there for me. When I'm sad he comes and comforts me by putting on my favorite music. He wraps his arms around me and says "So sweet, Dawson."

It's fun and exciting to have a brother with Down syndrome but sometimes it's tough. Garrett is also very impatient and strong which can lead to me getting hurt.

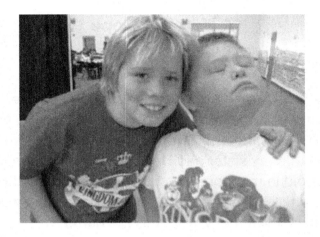

He is also very stubborn and yells a lot when he's mad. Overall, I think having him in my life is much more positive than negative and if I had the choice to take away his Down Syndrome ~ I wouldn't because I think he's perfect just the way he is.

Garrett and I bounce on the trampoline and wrestle together. Even though I'm a year and a half older than Garrett, he usually beats me in wrestling.

A story that I remember is one time when I was really sad. I was sitting in the room talking to my mom and didn't want anyone else to be in the room with us. But, Garrett came in anyway and saw that I was very upset. Garrett went and turned on music that I love and he snuggled up next to me and told me he loves me.

I think the most beautiful thing about Garrett is the sweetness in his heart.

A Hero for Hope

Written by: Hannah Wang

My name is Hannah. I am 7 years old. I have a sister who has Down syndrome named Hope. She is almost 5 years old. We live in Markham, Ontario, Canada. My parents found out that my sister had Down syndrome when she was 13 weeks old in my mommy's tummy. They knew there would be challenges ahead but they believed she was a gift from God, just like me. We picked the name Hope because we wanted to remember that we would always have hope in Jesus and I wanted her to have the same initial as me!

Hope was very cute during the first two years. She was quiet and liked to smile. She was very chubby and I liked to squeeze her face. I enjoyed playing with her until she turned two. She couldn't speak and she threw a lot of tantrums. I felt like I was walking on egg shells all the time.

When she was about three years old, she started to scratch and pinch a lot. She scratched me because she wanted something but she didn't know how to say it. Sometimes when I was playing the piano, she pushed me because she wanted to play. Sometimes we were playing together nicely, and for no reason she would scratch me. Occasionally the scratch was so bad that it made me bleed or the pinch was so hard that I got a horrible bruise. For almost a year I had nightmares almost every day about her hurting me. I woke up crying and became very nervous and fearful of her. It took us two years to finally see her behavior improve.

Her speech has improved over the past year. However, there are still times when we don't understand her. If we ask her to say it again and we still don't understand her, we get frustrated and so does she. There are times that she gets angry and throws things around which can hit people around her. So we have to be really careful! One time I was trying to teach her Rainbow Loom. She told me she did not want my help so I did not help her. But she did not make it clear that she did not even want me to be there. Then, she hit my head with the loom. Her speech delay has caused a lot of frustrations and problems between us.

Hope and I like to play together. Our favorite game is pretend play. We pretend that we are camping, grocery shopping, taking care of dolls, and riding on a bus or an airplane. I have to finish my homework before I get to play with her. Sometimes, she can't wait and becomes impatient or throws a tantrum. I want to play with her, too. This motivates me to finish my homework fast! When she behaves well during our play, I am willing to give up making Rainbow Loom bracelets!

Hope likes music. She likes to create her own way of playing music. She sometimes strikes her tambourine against her thigh and plays the harmonica at the same time. She sings and dances and wants us to watch her because she thinks she is performing. I think she is so cute.

My mommy takes us to a nursing home regularly to visit the seniors as volunteers. I don't feel comfortable in their rooms because of the smell, but Hope doesn't care. She goes right in to find a senior in bed or in a chair. She touches or even kisses their hands. I can handle the smell and will go in with her but I still don't like it. Sometimes, I just stand there and my sister comes and calls me to dance together. The seniors enjoy our singing and dancing and often smile and request for more. Sometimes if they know the song, they clap their hands and sing along. I think it is Hope's beauty that she is not scared of the seniors and she brings them joy with her cuteness.

One night when we were going to sleep, she lay down beside me. She sang this lullaby that my mother made up when I was small using the tune of "Are you sleeping, Brother John". She sang " blankie, blankie, blankie, blankie, I am fine? I am fine? blankie, blankie, blankie, blankie, I am fine? I am fine?" But it was supposed to be "blankie, blankie, blankie, blankie, how are you? How are you? blankie, blankie, blankie, blankie, I am fine? I am fine?" It was very sweet that she was trying to put me to sleep with her version of the lullaby.

One time, I was crying and Hope had just learned to walk around that time. She crawled all the way upstairs to a room, got a tissue and crawled all the way back down because she only knew where to get the tissue from one room upstairs. She gave it to me and tried to comfort me by hugging me. At that time, she was still small. She made me feel warm. Even though she is older now, she still makes me feel warm. She still comes to hug me or give me an ice pad when I am sad or when I get hurt. She wants to help comfort me even if I don't need it. Sometimes, that annoys me but most of the time it warms my heart.

We visited Hong Kong last year. One day, we went to a park near my grandparents' apartment. Hope went on a slide and was about to slide down. A boy who was younger than her pushed her from the back. She was scared. She went down and the boy followed her down. She tried to stay away from him by riding on a bouncy horse but the boy went near her and pushed her down. She went to another one and the boy continued to follow her. But, then, I blocked him! This time the boy was scared and ran away. Even though Hope often treated me poorly during that period, I was upset that she got bullied by another kid. I was glad that I was able to save her as her bigger sister. That was the first time I felt I was her hero and would protect her.

One night Hope was sleeping and I was lying beside her getting ready to sleep. I was scared that there might be a bad person coming from the window, I didn't want my sister to get caught so I held her hand. I wanted to protect her. I hope I can still live with her when I grow up. I think she might need my help with her life and I would like to help her. If she doesn't have a job and can't make money, at least, I can share some money with her so she can live and enjoy her life because I don't want to see her suffer. I hope she won't scratch people anymore when she grows up. I think it is possible she won't, if I continue to teach her and be kind to her. I love her very much.

My Sister is Special

Written by: Emma Barnett

My little sister Mallory has Down syndrome. She's two years old. Mallory is not as strong as us.

She can crawl. Mallory is beginning to hold onto things to help her stand up. She is not able to walk yet. Mallory does not know how to talk.

When my sister goes to Down syndrome of Louisville I go too. While there she learns how to do different things.

Mallory is learning how to sing and clap during circle time. She gets to play with some dolls.

My mom also pushes her on the swing. Mallory likes to play at the corn table.

My sister is very special to me. She gives me lots of hugs and kisses. I like to snuggle with my sister.

We watch Mickey Mouse together. My sister is very special!

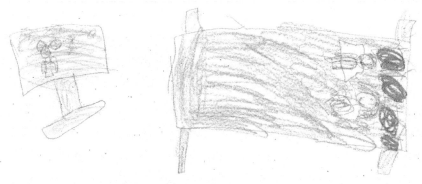

My Good Scar

Written by: Jake Fitzgerald

I am Jake Fitzgerald. I am the oldest of 4 kids. I am 13, Dawson is 11, Garrett is 10 and Carly is 6. Garrett was born with Down syndrome.

One time in the middle of my class, the front office called me down because they needed me to help with Garrett. I went down to the office and talked with Garrett a little bit and told him that I was counting on him to do the right thing. Garrett got up and did what he was supposed to do. It made me feel good ~ like I have a secret connection with him.

One day my brother Dawson and I were fighting, Garrett came out at us and yelled at us ~ first at me ~ and said a lot of words I couldn't quite understand but ended with a clear "NO FIGHT!" And then he ran into the room where Dawson was  and repeated the same words, ending with "NO FIGHT!" He repeated those same words to each of us about 5 times until we stopped fighting. We did it for Garrett.

A fun memory of Garrett is when he would play a classical song that was very dramatic over and over and over and over! He would dance around in a circle and express with his dancing what he felt the music was saying. He's a BIG music lover and is eclectic in his taste for music. He likes Rascal Flatts, Bill Maloney, and most pop and classical music.

I like having a brother with Down syndrome because now I have a different perspective from a lot of other people. Having Garrett in my life has taught me how to care for my brother and I would hope it has helped me care for others, as well.

It's fun to have Garrett in our family because everyone freaks out a little when they first see him but, once they spend time with Garrett, they become protective and defensive of him. They want to make sure others don't feel the same way they felt when they first met him. It's also hard at times, because Garrett runs away. We get really scared when we don't know if he's safe or not.

The two things I love about Garrett the most are that he is really nice and super funny. He makes our family laugh all the time. He's got some great dance moves, and he can sing loud. He's also the king of funny faces and KNOWS how to charm an audience.

Here is a poem I wrote in 4th grade. Our assignment was to write about a scar.

My Scar

When someone asks me if I have a scar I tell them I do, but it isn't in sight. I have one but you can't see it. It's invisible. A scar is something permanent. It stays in your life forever. My scar came home from a hospital in October. October 18, 2003. My scar will be a lifelong companion. Those few days after my scar was made were full of looks, gasps, silences. "It looks funny." "Ewwww." My scar was produced by two important people, two very important people in my life. Other people told me it was a bad thing. Family told me it was a good thing. I didn't know. My story, my exhilarating story. Sometimes kids at school make fun of my scar. I don't like it. They don't know how great it is to have my scar. My brother with Down syndrome-Garrett. I never said all scars are bad. My scar will stay with me forever. And that's how I want it to be.

Little Angel Landon

Written by: Hannah Bordon

In February of 2010 my little angel on earth, also known as my little brother, was born. Little did we know he had Down syndrome. Landon, my little brother, was born when I was 11. We didn't know he had DS until after he was born. I didn't know much about DS so I thought little about it and put together in my head that it wasn't that big of a deal.

Before Landon turned 1 he had three open heart surgeries within one week. The first couple months were anything but normal. I thought I was supposed to have a little brother screaming and crying each night but I had a little brother that was in the hospital. I don't remember when he first got out of the hospital, but I do remember my life changing, and now I see that it changed for the absolute best.

From there everything was a little more "normal". It was just like having any other baby in the house until he started to grow. The more he grew the more I noticed he was different. When it came time for him to start talking he would only grunt and make gestures that we would only know what they meant. With some speech and physical therapy he started to talk a ton more and get a lot quicker on his feet.

Over the past year I can't count how many perfume bottles have been broken because Landon is so sneaky. He can get into my room and get into everything. That little cutie does the damage of a tornado. Landon got accepted to preschool this past year and he loves it. He has made so many friends. Landon now attends the preschool I went to when I was his age. All the teachers love him. Just recently a lady at his school said he is probably ready for big boy underwear which means no more pull ups and that is a big accomplishment for him.

Over this past year Landon has learned to talk so much, as a matter of fact, I don't think he knows how to stop talking. I've laughed so hard I cry a countless number of times because of the cute things he would say unexpectedly.

Landon's favorite thing to do is dance. The first thing he says when I walk through the door is "sissy dance, please." How can you turn that down, so of course I dance with him! One time we had our own little routine to Starships by Niki Minaj. This also consists of singing Katy Perry and Georgia Florida songs.

The past 4 years have been so much fun with my little buddy. Landon is probably my best friend and, of course, my little angel.

My Sister Tuisku

Written by: Taika Sorensen

"Can we go outside Äiti?" I asked hopefully. "Sure." My sister and I raced outside. We thought about what to play for a long time. Finally, we decided to play "Dora". Then we had to agree on who got to be which character. "Wait, Tuisku, we need to ask Aku if he can play with us." "Why does Aku need to play?" my sister, Tuisku, asked curiously. "Because he needs to be Diego." I answered confidently. In the end, we agreed that I would be Boots the monkey, and Tuisku would be Dora. We even succeeded in persuading my brother, Aku, to play. I bet you're wondering why that would be a task. It's because he was eight then and already thought he was too old to play Dora. In spite of that, he loved us enough to give in.

We had a blast; "Oh no, Dora, I'm falling!" I cried as I slid down our slide. "I'll save you! Hold on to the swing! Wait, the swing is stuck." Tuisku said as she tried to lift the heavy swing over the side of the slide. "Aku, can you help me?" Tuisku asked. I burst into a fit of giggles. "I think the game is on pause." I said through my giggles, as my brother helped Tuisku. My mom saw Aku helping Tuisku and called out: "Aku make sure you don't do it for her, either do it with Tuisku, or show her how to do it, then let her try." "I know, I know." Aku called back. And he did know. Even I knew, and I was only two back then. Although I was two and my sister was three years older, there were still some things that I had already learned to do, but my sister was still learning. Every time I helped Tuisku when I was little, I got the same short lecture from my mom, and I still do.

Now, before I go onto telling you about another time when I had so much fun with Tuisku, let me tell you about our family. First, I'll tell you some things about myself:

I love gymnastics, violin, piano, musicals, reading, math, animals, singing, and acting. However, what I love most is my friends and family. My brother loves being in charge, talking, violin, conducting, music, and orchestra. My mom loves singing, piano, her homeland (Finland), and black licorice. My dad loves ice cream, musicals, singing, listening to music, and computers. My sister loves chocolate, singing, ice cream, dancing, cello, reading, writing, art, and little kids. You see, we all love similar *and* different things, and that is what makes us special, but there is one more thing that makes my sister special. That's because she has Down syndrome.

Down syndrome is a disability that in most cases is caused by an extra chromosome 21, for a total of 47 chromosomes, instead of 46. Some common effects of Down Syndrome are heart problems, thyroid problems, developmental problems, eye problems, hearing problems, and mental retardation. I bet you're thinking, *Boy, that's a lot of problems. Can she do anything?* Well, if I guessed correctly, the answer is a: "Yeah, duh!" I hope that doesn't sound rude, but believe me, I've heard some of the meanest things about Tuisku. The people don't know I'm her sister, because we don't really look alike, so everybody talks about her to my face. "Wow, she's ugly!" "Look, she's so slow." "What on earth is the matter with her?" "She talks so weird." These are some of the comments I hear. My mom always tells me: "Just make up a good comeback, you're good at those." "Oh, so she's ugly and you're not?" "Look, she can

actually do things correctly, by taking her time. Unlike you."
"What on earth is the matter with you?" "I know, so do you."

Here's another story:

"Girls, you're supposed to be getting ready for bed." My mom called to us from the living room. "Okay!" I tried to call back to her, but I couldn't, because I was laughing so hard. "Hey Tuisku, let try another thing that might make you laugh." I said to her, after we finished laughing and began to continue brushing our teeth. "Uh-oh. Taika, you know you don't need to experiment to find out how to make me laugh. You're really funny no matter what!" Tuisku replied. "No really," I said. "One more thing." "Alright." "PINK, FLUFFY UNICORNS!!!" I bellowed. Tuisku burst out laughing, and laughed for a really long time. "Girls, I said bed!!!!" my mom called again. "OKAY!" We both called back, and burst into another round of giggles, but this time we were able to make it to bed.

And that, my friend, is my sister Tuisku.

What is better than One? Two!

Written by: Ellie Goulding

It's cool to think that I have TWO siblings with Down syndrome, but sometimes it can get a little crazy. Charity (8) and Neko (5) bring lots of joy and happiness to me. Well, with Charity we've taken a wild ride in the hospital, when her heart stopped twice, she went into cardiac arrest, and had open heart surgery. So as you can see, she is a miracle baby!!!! As for Neko, he has had a little less excitement. He did have a seizure and that is something Charity has not gone through!

Well as you can see, both Charity and Neko have had no ordinary lives!!!!

One of their favorite things to do is when we do what Charity, Neko, and I call "music." It is when I teach them about numbers, letters, animals, and many other things all to MUSIC!!!!!! Charity sometimes is in her own little world, but when she comes back to our world from her world, she realizes that there are people in the room then she goes " hi oie " (that is what she calls me instead of Ellie). Charity is full of singing - she sings in the car, she sings in the house, and she sings at the top of her lungs right after she's eaten her fill at the dinner table! Charity is her own little bunch of love!! Going down the line to........NEKO, well that kid is a bundle of everything!! He is the baby of the house so he is always being kissed, loved on, and held. I want Neko to have a VERY close relationship with me, but sometimes he prefers boys better (because, of course, he's a BOY).

Charity and Neko are both adopted, but if we choose to obey God we will also be adopted into a perfect family!!! Neko and Charity are a huge blessing to me, they have taught me to love and brighten anyone's and everyone's day!!! I now adore "Down syndrome" because of my TWO awesome siblings!!!!!

My Penny

Written by: Ruby Parksion

My name is Ruby. I am 5 years old. My sister is 7. Her name is Penny. I want to give her a hug and I want to play with her, and she's really a little bit crazy, and I want to move her around, and I want to play her favorite game and her favorite game is "Ariel" and, I want to play with no one.

I like to go to the museum with her. I like to change her diaper and I like to spank her if she does anything or climbing and I like to play at the playground with her and I like to have a party with her and I like to sing happy birthday to Penny and me too, and I want to share the cake with her.

Tanner

Written by: Madison Winjum

Hi, I'm Madison Winjum. I'm here to talk about my little brother, Tanner; he is only 7 years old. And he is only 42 pounds. And, honestly, sometimes it's a little hard. You see, Tanner was born with Down syndrome and he had a stunning 13 holes in his heart! And he only weighed I pound. He went through many surgeries, my parents and him had to go to the hospital probably every week. It probably cost a lot, but it was definitely worth it…

My dad took Tanner fishing, and Tanner alone (with a little help from dad) pulled in a 48in. and 12 lbs. Northern Pike! That's pretty good for him! Tanner might not be like most kids, but I think it's a blessing he's not. He does things with you that lots of other kids can't do. And just because he has Down syndrome doesn't mean he's different. And if he is, he's different in a good way.

When we go to church every Sunday and we're in the middle of church, he will want other people to hold him and we might not even know them! Also when we leave, he will want to walk with everyone and hold their hands; he always puts a smile on their faces!

I always kind of knew he had DS. Sometimes I get mad at him, but at the end of the day I remember he has DS, and his problems are probably worse than mine. I couldn't imagine life without him. We have the most amazing dog, Inksly (and yes his name is Inksly), and Tanner could do anything to him and Inksly wouldn't care.

Has anyone ever told you it's rude to stare? Well if they have, it's true. It is rude to stare. It might be hard, and even once in a while I catch myself off guard. It could get the people you're staring at mad, sad, and maybe even embarrassed. Whenever we go out in public with Tanner, since he has Downs, he might look different to other people. And they stare and stare and stare. And that really gets on my nerves. I always tell my mom, and then she says, "Other people may have never seen someone like Tanner". It calms me down a little but I'm still pretty mad.

When Tanner was little he couldn't swallow so, he had a G-tube going into his stomach and that's how we fed him for a while. Then when we were going downstairs, his G-tube fell out. So, we had to go to the hospital. It was about a 5-hour wait. He was drinking well enough that we didn't have to put it back in. Then after a couple years he could eat baby food and he still only eats baby food and milk.

My Fun Adventure

Written by: Aubrie Reid (8 years old)

Having a sister with Down syndrome is an adventure for everyone. It may take longer for her to learn our games, but that's okay. Instead she is fun to sit by and let her hug. She's a lot of fun! Ollie is curious & funny and we are so happy to have her.

Lots of Fun

Written by: Harrison Goulding

Hi, my name is Harrison and I have two siblings with Down syndrome, and I'd like to share with you about them – their names are Charity and Neko.

Charity has taught me a lot of things; she taught me how to swing toys, and it's a lot of fun to play with her. She taught me how fun it is to swing swings.

And also Neko, who has Down syndrome, he taught me how to play with friends and be a better friend. They always taught me how to do fun things together. And the thing I like about Charity and Neko is that Charity, she loves me a lot and she bosses me around and its super funny. And Neko he loves to play with me a lot – it's a lot of fun!

My Sunshine Boy

Written by: Rachelle Chavez

I have a little brother with Down syndrome and his name is Joaquin. He was born on February 23, 2013. He has lots of brown hair and hazel eyes. When I found out that Joaquin had Down syndrome I didn't know what it meant but I still loved him no matter what. The next day the doctor explained to us what Down syndrome was. The doctor said it means he has an extra chromosome and it would take him longer to do things and he would look different. I looked at him but he didn't look different to me. He had two eyes, one nose, two ears, lips like me and Daddy and born with lots of hair like me and Mommy. I called him my sunshine boy because he made me smile. He's my favorite person in the whole wide world.

My favorite moment is when I held him for the first time. I was in the room when he was born. Another favorite time is when we had his Baptism at our church. I was so proud. At night we do our prayers  and I help hold his hands together. I love my brother's laugh and when he yells silly words and sounds. We really like reading together and our favorite book is "We'll Paint the Octopus Red."

Things changed in my family when Joaquin came home. He became everyone's favorite! He was so tiny when he was born he had to use a carbed instead of a carseat for a whole month! I enjoy learning about Down syndrome. I write stories about my baby brother in class to teach others about Down syndrome. I'm so proud of him. I like going to his therapy to learn new ways to help teach him new things. He has mild hearing loss and wears baby hearing aids and I am learning sign language. He is army crawling and sitting up for five minutes. It might take him longer to learn things but he can and will do anything.

My brother's name is Joaquin Xavier Chavez and he has Down syndrome Power!

Captivating stories of life with siblings who have Down syndrome

High School/College Age Siblings

The Harsh Words

Written by: Anonymous

The harsh words of the doctor, nearly pierced your heart

He'll never amount to much, he says

Give him up, institutionalize him.

You decide to keep him, unsure how you would survive

Would he ever bring you happiness?

But now you know

The doctor should've told you

How much you'd grow from this child

And how much he would teach you.

And that although he would struggle

To perform the simplest of actions,

When he succeeds, you will get great happiness.

And you wonder now

Why all they told you was the negative

Instead of focusing on the good

Kristiana – A True Blessing

Written by: Marissa Contreras

Hi my name is Marissa, I'm 19. I have a baby sister named Kristiana, and she is 10. When I found she had Down syndrome, I didn't understand until my mom explained to me her disability. I've never looked at her differently, but I've learned a lot while she was growing up. Because of her, I'm a better person. She has taught me passions. She's a true blessing my sister. Growing up it was difficult. People would stare and say rude things about my sister. But you learn to push it to the side. I thank God a lot for giving me a sister with Down syndrome. She cheers me up when I'm sad. She showed me things differently. I see in her eyes. She's a blessing. She amazes me a lot. Each day she gets smarter and smarter. Never did I think about my daily life until she was born. I see the whole world differently. She's difficult sometimes-she has her days-but we learn to work through it. We have had our scares with her but it brought us closer.

The biggest thing my sister has taught me was how to see everyone the same, even with a disability. I never thought anything of it until my sister was born. That is when I started to see everything the way she sees it. She teaches me new little things every day. I love and appreciate her in my life. She's my little blessing. One thing I love to do with my sister is to cuddle up with her and watch movies. She always

loves that. She's so funny during movies. Her reactions from some movies are funny. It's little moments like that I cherish. I remember the day she was born they told me we have to be very careful with her because she had downs. We always feared she would have cancer. She always got tested. We loved her so much- how could our nana bear get it? We feared a little bit that she was going to have it, but we found out she's cancer free. She didn't have it. I love my sister a lot, and losing her would break my heart so much.

My Brother Nick

Written by: Hank Unnerstall

My brother Nick is not like any ordinary brother. There is an extra chromosome in the 21st pair, which is the result of Nick having Down syndrome and later, an autism diagnosis that separates him from normal people. Having Nick as a brother has made me open my eyes to life in general and the traits that make me the man I am today.

Some of the earliest memories with Nick start from when I was around 5 years old. Being that young, I did not fully understand why my brother was different but I accepted it because he is my brother. I remember

when I began getting older and going to elementary school when my mom and brother would pick me up and drop me off at school. Nick would be doing his normal sound making and hand clapping in public that would sometimes embarrass me in front of my peers. I also recall the times at the old California house we had where Nick and I would start messing around and wrestling with each other but then Nick would take it seriously and start pinching me. His ways of fighting back around that time were much less harmful than it is now when he has one of his meltdowns or I like to call them "monkey boy" episodes. These memories are some examples of tough things I have had to deal with growing up with my brother.

It would be remiss of me if I didn't mention a horribly embarrassing time. Back around my freshman year of high school, Nick and his respite worker and I all went to Arby's for a late lunch. Once we got our food we sat down, Nick started to make loud and disgruntled sounds when we put his food in front of him. I told him to be quiet in a not so nice tone. Next thing you know he became furious and proceeded to throw his food and random objects like trays, sugar packets and salt shakers all over the place. We tried to calm him down but he was at the point of no return (aka monkey boy.) I went on to restrain him and he was pinching, kicking and biting, anything to hurt me. Somehow we ended wrestling around on the ground and, to the other people in the restaurant, it must have looked like we were fighting. This was awkward and embarrassing for me because I was much bigger than him. I knew it didn't look right. I just wanted to leave and never show my face again.

That was the worst, or well at least one of them!

But, there are many traits to Nick. For example, he is usually a very happy and silly kid who always has a grin on his face. That's why people love him at school and, of course, our family, despite what we deal with when relating to Nick. Also, even though Nick has autism, it does not stop him from being a socially engaging little dude even though he can't speak. He loves to get attention whether it is him trying to act cute or to negatively do something to get ours. For example if we do not pay Nick any attention for awhile he might spray shaving cream over the stairs.

Some of the best memories I can recall having with my brother can be the times where he will just sit next to me on the couch and watch TV with me and just chill out. Also I love to see him dance intensely while listening to the music that I provide him which is usually hip-hop/rap. Basically, whenever Nick is in a good mood and happy he always knows how to put a smile on my face, and the faces of many other people. Having Nick as a brother has taught me to be a very patient person. I think I got this trait from the numerous times I have had to babysit Nick throughout the years. Also, I feel that I have a certain outlook on life after growing up with Nick. For instance, Nick is always happy about the smallest things and he's the one with the disability. So now I've been trying to live my life to the fullest, and I'm always trying to be as positive as possible no matter what life throws at me.

Frank and the Ups and Downs

Written by: Jennifer Krull

My name is Jennifer, and I am fifteen years old. I have one sibling, named Frank who has Down syndrome. He is twenty years old.

Having a sibling with Down syndrome has its ups and downs, as does anything. Some people may view my brother as "different", even though he is just like you and me. I can become annoyed with my brother when he constantly repeats things, or says his famous "I'm a big kid" saying. But if needed, I will stand up for him and protect him when others are being rude. I will admit that I get frustrated when my friends talk about doing things with their "normal" siblings that I can never do with mine. Sometimes I wish that I could have a "normal" sibling. However, I would not trade anything in for Frank. I also dislike it when people use the word "retarded". It offends me in a way

most people do not understand. If they walked in my shoes for one day, then they might think twice about using "the word".

Frank is a very active kid. He participates in many sports, including baseball, soccer, and basketball. I enjoy volunteering to help the children who participate. We share many fun memories, and do many activities together. Frank loves going on roller coasters with me at amusement parks, and he likes to help me make gifts for our family members around holidays and birthdays. Two of Frank's favorite things to do are dancing and reading. At my cousin's wedding, he was the first person on the dance floor. Frank got the party started, and soon it seemed like all of the guests were on the dance floor with him. He always seems to have his nose in a book, and he loves it when I read to him.

Frank is pleasant, but not overly social. He enjoys life, and never expresses any negativity toward others. He can always cheer me up if I am having a bad day. I will always be a major part of Frank's life, even through the ups and downs. I have learned from him that life is fragile and I should try to enjoy every second of it. I should be thankful for the things that I have and not take anything for granted. Frank has shaped me into a better person, and I have learned much from him. I am thankful to have him in my life, and would not be the person I am today without him.

Lil' Ian for Ya'

Written by: Keegan Halter

Having a little brother with Down syndrome is really, really difficult, stressful, brilliant, rewarding, and life-changing. When I first found out I had a brother I was ecstatic; I had always wanted a sibling and now I finally had one! When I found out he had Down syndrome I denied it; although I did not quite understand what it meant, I was just glad to have a sibling. Over time I began to understand that Ian learned a little slower than I did, and I learned what having a brother really meant. I had to take care of him more than a couple times, and watching Ian was not usually high on my list of wants at the time.

Having a brother with Down syndrome can be one of the best things in the world or one of the worst; when Ian was mad he was very mad, and he could even be quite hurtful at times. But when he was happy or when someone got hurt he became one of the sweetest and most kind people in the entire world. Ian is more open with his emotions than other people, and one of the things I like most is that he is not very complicated. Do not get me wrong - he is really intelligent but he is more open and clear in knowing what he wants and why. For example; if he wants something he tells you, if he does not he lets you know, an ability which I think a lot of people in the world are lacking and, in my opinion, people's lives would often be a lot better if they were more simple; that is not always the case but I think it is true fairly often.

Ian is a wonderful person; he is adorable, kind, caring, and very helpful at times. Whenever I felt depressed, sad, or just out of sorts I could go to Ian and spend some time with him. I did not talk about my troubles, I just tried to entertain him, and when I did I found that doing so had also made me feel better, too. Ian has been very supportive and helpful just by being himself, even when he is feeling out of sorts; he usually helps me deal with stress just by being the sweet and innocent person that he is. In fact, when he wants to spend time with you, he'll say, "Little Ian for ya'." Do not get me wrong, having a brother with Down syndrome can be very stressful and frustrating, but I believe the good points more than make up for it. Those with Down syndrome are people, just as kind, happy, jealous, excitable, angry, good, bad, and beautiful as other people, they just learn slower and are more open with their emotions.

To summarize, my brother is an incredible and wonderful human being, he can be grouchy, but he has a very big heart and will do his best to help others. From my limited experience with other children who have Down syndrome, they appear to have about the same attitude. I believe getting to know someone with Down syndrome can be a very enlightening and amazing experience. I can honestly say that without my brother I would be a different person, likely for the worse.

EDITOR'S NOTE: The title "Little Ian for ya'" is not misspelled; this is exactly what Ian says to us. Ian and his brother are 7 years apart.

Double the Fun

Written by: Linsey Strolberg

My name is Linsey Strolberg, I'm 19 years old, and I have two older biological brothers, my only siblings. Luke, who's 20, has Autism, and Levi, 21, has Down syndrome.

I love my brothers! They have taught me important skills that are now, and forever will, help me in my life. From patience to family values. I'll always be grateful to my brothers.

Levi and I are really close. I love Luke just as much, but he likes to keep to himself, as most Autistic people do, but Levi is really social. When I pick him up from work he gives his co-workers high fives and a big smile before he leaves. After work he loves to watch the T.V. show "Barney". Thanks to him I probably know every Barney song created. I sing along to the episodes sometimes as he watches them, even though I can't carry a decent note to save my life.

Levi is non-verbal, so he makes "eeing" noises, groans, and humming noises most of the time. Whenever he watches football he gets so excited, like, I don't even know how to describe it. He sounds extremely happy when the players tackle. Doesn't matter what team, as long as there is a lot of tackling. He makes a loud "Gee!" sound when he's super happy.

A majority of the time Levi is easy going. He's a homebody, so it can be difficult sometimes to try and get him out of the house. If he gets cranky he'll make an annoyed "eeing" or hum. If he isn't cooperating, then Luke will make him, and that's when he gets very cranky, and becomes louder. When we're out in public and Levi starts to get cranky, or if there's a baby crying he'll cry in sympathy for it, people start staring. When I was between the ages of 11-14, it bothered me a lot that people stared at my brothers. Like it was some big spectacle that Levi is crying, and Luke is gripping his arm. I felt like telling all the parents that didn't discipline their bawling kids because the kid doesn't understand the word "No", that the only reason my brother started to cry and make a big scene is because of your parenting skills. Obviously, I didn't say anything, but once Levi started crying then the kid, or kids would stop crying and stare at my brother, then the parents would stare. It's like "Really? Stop! Stop and continue with your day. Just go away please!"

When I turned 15 I didn't let people get to me as bad, but then, once I got into high school, a majority of the students didn't know my brothers had a younger sister. I started getting questions like "How do you handle them?" or "Is it hard living with them?" I just told them "I don't think it's hard whatsoever." I've grown up with them, I don't know any different from a-typical "Normal Family Life" to what my family is called. My parents have gotten the comments "Oh, you're that kind of family." Or "You have those kind of children." What do those people mean? My brothers never begged for money, they'll never have to be bailed out of jail because it won't cross their minds to steal something, or go shoot someone, they won't get any girl pregnant, and they don't have the urge to drink and party it up every weekend. As of right now my family sounds more "normal" than most of America's families.

Living with people who have disabilities can be difficult, but every day is rewarding, and I love my brothers a little more each day. I mean, what's not to love? Luke is full of life and energy, and Levi is a giant teddy bear that warms your heart. How is that hard to live with?

Hate Cannot Win

Written by: Aaron Rapp, 2011 (18 years)

Last August, I was texting a (cute) girl I had just met. In passing I mentioned that my sister had Down syndrome. I remember almost dropping my phone in shock when she replied "I'm so sorry that must be a huge hindrance for you." My sister has been many things to me: an inspiration, a teacher, a friend, but never a hindrance. It can be a shock to encounter the way the outside world perceives those with disabilities.

Eden, my sister, was born with Trisomy 21, or Down syndrome, one of the most common forms of mental retardation on the planet. As soon as she was born, my mom became very involved in the disability community, and because Eden is only three and a half years younger than me, I was immersed as well. Society as a whole shuns and mocks people with disabilities. I suppose it is because people fear those who are different. That is why people with disabilities are the largest unchurched demographic in the United States. When people see my sister, they don't always see what I see: a sweet teenage girl, full of personality, made in the image of God. Too often they see someone whose brain moves slower, someone who talks funny, a "retard." Who would want to go to church with a "retard?"

Jesus would.He said it himself in Luke 14: "When you give a banquet, invite the poor, the crippled, the lame, the blind, and you will be blessed. Although they cannot repay you, you will be repaid at the resurrection of the righteous," (Luke 14:13-14).

Unfortunately, the disability community is not the only people group that faces persecution in America. In the wake of September 11, 2001, Anti-Arab and Anti-Muslim sentiments filled the air. People needed a scapegoat, and many Middle Eastern people felt the heat. I'm proud to say that many in my church tried to counteract the hate and suspicion before it was too late. Because I attended a Japanese Church, we knew the effects of angered retaliation all too well.

In 1942, shortly after the attack on Pearl Harbor, President Roosevelt signed Executive Order 9066, which forced Japanese Americans into internment camps for the rest of the war. Several of the older members of my church can recall firsthand the experience of the camps: being stripped of not only their rights as loyal Americans, but also of their basic human rights.

The Japanese community refused to let another group

suffer what they had to bear. Hate is a very real part of the world. Some people will judge you because of your race or your appearance. If I have learned anything from my sister, it is that as long as we try to make the world a better place, the hate cannot win.

Here is a short story I wrote about my sister when I was 8 years old

My five-year-old sister Eden is special. She has Down syndrome, which is when an extra twenty-first chromosome comes in and acts like a brake to slow things down. Only 1 in 800-1000 infants have Down syndrome. But having Down syndrome isn't the only way Eden is special.

When anyone needs help, she's always there to lend a hand. When anybody asks for help, she excitedly smiles and says, "Yes!" and she does it. When she helps me pick up my room, she never stops for long. But the ways Eden is special doesn't stop there.

Eden is very loving. When anyone is upset or feeling down, she'll sit by them and comfort them. First she comes up and squats near them and tries to catch their eye. And then she opens her arms wide and hugs them or pats them. My mom has told me when something sad happens in a picture book, Eden sometimes pats the illustrations or kisses it. And if someone is hurt she always kindly asks, "What happened?"

So in many ways and a lot more that I haven't had time to mention, Eden is very special. And I'm happy Eden is my sister.

Frankie

Written by: Dominic Gentile

"Happy birthday, dear Dominic, happy birthday to you!"

"Ready to help Dommy blow out the candles, Frankie?"

"No. Hap' bir' 'oo yooOOO!"

"We sang it already!" " 'Gainnnn!"

"Frank, we already sang it twice, it's time to help Dominic blow out the candles."

And before I can take a breath, half of my birthday candles are blown out.

For the 14th year in a row.

But it's okay, because his smile is better than any wish I could ever make.

My name is Dominic; I am 20 years old and the first-born of my parents, Fran and Janice. For the first three years of my life, I reigned as only child and pretty much the center of my parents' attention. But when I was four, my mom gave birth to triplets. Overnight, my family doubled in size. I went from an only child to one of four, from a family of three to a family of six. Kaitlin, Nicholas, and Colleen entered my life and I no longer had the luxury of being the only child. After a few years, and a few trips to the family therapist, I got over it. But, if that wasn't exciting enough, two years later my mom had Frankie, my youngest brother, who was born with Down syndrome.

I don't remember exactly when my parents told me that Frankie wasn't going to be "normal." As a young kid, I guess I just accepted that Frankie was going to be different and that this "different" was going to be his normal. I don't remember a time thinking Frankie was not going to be an average kid nor do I remember a time of being sad because Frankie had Down syndrome. I do, however, remember two things: a book and a simple question.

First was the children's book <u>Paint the Octopus Red</u>. This book is about a little girl learning how to adjust to having a new baby brother with Down syndrome in her family. I remember Mom bringing it home and sitting me down to read it with her. This book was the first time that I was introduced to what it might be like to have a sibling with special needs. In the book, a little girl helps her brother do things like play with toys and eat his snacks and paint. She quickly learns that her brother cannot do things as fast as she can or he may do them differently, like painting a picture of an octopus red instead of purple. In the end, she realizes she needs to accept that he does things differently and she loves him for it. Mom and I talked about how Frankie would be different from the triplets (Although even that situation wasn't considered normal either!) and other kids, too. She explained to me how our lives would be different after Frankie was born. She explained to me that he might act, look, or think differently than us, but no matter what, we will always love and help him.

As a young six-year-old, I started to imagine the ways I would help my new baby brother, just like the little girl in the book. I would teach him how to play Legos, how to dance to the Lawrence Welk Show, and how to play on the playground. I also started to create some very interesting scenarios in my mind. I, as Frankie's older brother, had to be his protector. I started to think what would happen if Frankie was being bullied by a bunch of kids. What would I do? I imagined myself surrounded by four older kids picking on Frankie. I pictured myself running in and knocking all four of them out and saving Frankie, like the super hero brother I would be. Thank goodness I never had to do that, mostly because the likelihood of me winning in a fight is not so great. But I did start to realize that Frankie would not be living a normal life. He may walk different, talk different, or look different, but I would still need to be his big brother.

Secondly, I remember when I asked my parents, "Did you cry when you found out he had Down syndrome?" They responded, "Yes." As a six-year-old I could not comprehend why they would cry. I thought having a baby was something to be happy about—did they not want Frankie? I remember my mom telling me they cried because he wouldn't be able to do the things that "normal" kids could do. And I remember thinking, are they sad he won't be President of the Unites States or an astronaut? Because not many of us will be the President! I understand now why my parents cried—not because their hopes and dreams for their new son were considered impossible but because they knew how hard life would be for him. As a child, I didn't understand nor could I imagine the trials and obstacles Frankie would have to overcome in his life. My six-year-old mentality just thought about all of the cool things that we could do together!

Reflecting back, I guess I could say that I never really saw Down syndrome as a true disability, or something that doesn't let people live their lives. He would just be...different! Sure, being the older brother, I always tried to help him out, whether it was teaching him words, dances, or songs, sneaking him an extra cookie or help him open birthday presents. But I soon learned that he could do a lot of the day-to-day things that the rest of my siblings could do.

When Frankie was born, there were a lot of complications. My parents were in and out of the hospital all of the time. And when Dad had to work at night, Mom would stay in the hospital, which meant we needed to have a babysitter. So, we spent many nights under the careful watch of my Aunt Fran. One night in particular at my Aunt Fran's house, things were not looking too great for Frankie and we knew it. The triplets, four-years-old now, and I, a frightened little seven-year-old, were sleeping on the pull out bed. I remember one of them saying they missed Mom and Dad and another asking if Frankie was going to be okay. And I remember taking all three of them and huddling them close and reassuring them that everything was going to be okay, even if I didn't believe it myself.

Through those very tough first years, we became closer as a family. True, it took me awhile for me to really realize how much my family means to me but the bond was still there. I knew my family was always different I always just assumed it was because we had a big family of seven, and three of the kids were born at the same time and the other one looked weirdly cute. But looking back on it now, I think the trials we endured as a family (even if we did not completely understand them) and the help of our extended family, drove home the message of "family sticks together through thick and thin" at a young age. Not many kids have to see their parents try to deal with the stress of five kids under the age of six including a newborn in the hospital who is having one problem after the next. I think that's what made us different. We still fight and drive each other up a wall (actually, if you asked our parents they would tell you that's all we do) but we really do love each other and have a very special connection.

Today, Frankie is 14 years old and is in 6th grade. Frankie is a bit different from other kids with Down syndrome. Frankie has a hard time walking, so we have to use a wheelchair to get him from place to place, which can be a challenge at times. He cannot fully talk; he can make out a few syllables for simple words or he can use some sign language to communicate. Also, he's really overweight which, although it's part of the reason he is extremely cute, makes it even more difficult for him to walk. But these issues are easily overlooked when you meet my "Chubbs."

The first thing you notice when you meet Frankie is his smile. His smile is the definition of infectious. Making him laugh and giggle was so much fun as a kid and still is today! There was something about that big grin and his little chuckle that just lights up the entire room and everyone in it. I like to think his smile is somewhat of his secret weapon; he can get away with just about anything by flashing that deadly smile of his.

Frankie is also very destructive. Our playroom used to look like a war zone and many times it was because of him. He still loves to dump boxes out or knock toys over and just make a mess. And when you catch him in the act of dumping the bin of Legos for the third time that day, and you tell him sternly, "Don't you dare," Frankie will just giggle and, yet again, slowly dump the bin out while keeping eye contact and flashing his devilish smile. Once that happens, you can't help but smile and laugh with him.

Another talent Frankie is famous for is his dance moves. Man, can that kid rock out like it's nobody's business. Whether it is his favorite Barney or Wiggles video, or some song that comes on the radio, or even the sound of the blender, he loves to dance to it. Many family gatherings and parties, Frankie was, and still is, found in the middle of the dance floor, doing his "thang" and directing other people how to get down and get funky just like him. And if you aren't moving, he isn't afraid to pull you down to the floor and force you to do the crocodile with him. At family parties, it is no surprise to see my dad, my uncle Bob, and Frankie on their backs in the middle of the dance floor with their arms and legs ..... flailing in the air to Abba. No matter your age or dancing skill, no one is safe when Frankie is on the floor.

The most interesting and, quite frankly, surprising characteristic of Frankie is his intelligence and cleverness. Remember when I told you he has a hard time walking? Well, that's only half true. Within the last two years, we have been receiving video evidence from his aide at school that he is, in fact, a pretty good walker. On his own, he can walk up to 20 steps. But, from the way he acts at home, you would never know. Also, he is so smart at school. He can listen to a story and answer comprehensive questions on the stories and he even talks more too! But, because we tend to let him get away with not walking or talking at home, he knows how to work the system to make us work harder.

I have so many great stories of Frankie and his constant shenanigans.

One of my favorite memories of Frankie is from a few years ago. My parents decided to take me, my cousin Kelly, and Frankie out to dinner at a very nice restaurant. We got our seats and placed our order—Frankie got his usual mac n' cheese and my dad got a cheeseburger. When our food came, Frankie took one look at my dad's burger and declared he wanted it. Well, my dad, used to this ritual, told Frankie no, and to eat his mac n' cheese before it gets cold. Frankie, at this point, isn't too happy. He has made up his mind that he wants my dad's dinner and he knew he was going to get it.

Frankie looks at my dad, chuckles menacingly, and then lunges at the burger. My dad swiftly moves the burger out of Frankie's reach, and, out of anger, Frank starts grabbing whatever thing is closest to him—a plate of fries. My mom, foreseeing the impending catastrophe, reaches across the table to take the plate away from Frankie but, in a flash, he snatches the plate. They engage in a furious round of tug of war. Frustrated and angry, Frankie searches the table for the next best thing to throw—which so happened to be a fork. Frankie lets go of the plate, takes the fork and chucks it. It flies through the air across the table and lands right into my mom's head. The fork sticks right into the skin of her head and is now standing straight out of her head. My mom, in a state of shock, pulls the fork out of her head and just stares at Frankie in disbelief.

Kelly and I, meanwhile, are laughing so hard that tears are streaming down our faces. Frankie is still hurling everything in sight as my dad jumps out of the booth to grab Frankie's wheel chair and yanks Frankie out the booth. My mom is still sitting dumbfounded, still trying to process that she just pulled a fork out of her head. My dad gets Frankie into his chair but not before Frankie snatches his prize and chomps down on the burger right before my dad grabs it out of his hands and throws it back on the table. We all rush out of the restaurant, hoping that no one noticed the sounds of plates flying, grunts, laughs, and screams, but Frankie has one more idea for his big finish. He flips over a tray of dishes, hits a few unsuspecting patrons, and lets out a loud scream. The whole restaurant turns and stares at us.

Needless to say, we never returned to that restaurant again. Not only going out to restaurants, but going to the movies or to church or the mall is always a bit of a gamble with what will happen. Now, of course, it's no big deal to plop

Frankie into his wheel chair, and roll him around to wherever we go. But taking Frankie out and about is very telling on people.

Now, most time when we go out, there is generally a great response from people: the waiter who is willing to say hi especially to Frankie and shake his snotty hand and listen to his babbling even though my mom already ordered him a hot dog and a diet coke. There's the flight attendant who talks to Frankie about his Wiggles movie and asks him about his school. Or the woman at church who has no idea what the rest of my family's names are but never fails to come up to Frankie just to tell him he's her little angel and gives him a big hug and a kiss. Those great, beautiful, and kind responses to Frankie really make you smile and realize that there is good in the world.

But there are the very rare instances where you don't get that great of a response from people. Of course, there will always be the little kids, too young to understand that staring is rude. But then you come across the two teenagers at McDonald's who laugh right in Frankie's face because he looks different. Or when a whole family stops in their tracks to look at the chubby little boy yelling because he's excited to be at Disneyland. Then there are the groups of kids at a restaurant who stare at Frankie and may or may not take videos of him while we are enjoying a calm family dinner. Or the man on the plane who turns around and point blank tells my mom "I hope to God I never sit near you again" because Frankie was a little too loud on the plane.

I am fully aware that Frankie is not a perfect angel, but witnessing these things makes your blood boil. Sometimes I want to walk up to that person or that family and just scream—why do you have to stare? Did your parents not teach you that staring and pointing are rude? Do you not understand that he is a person? He is my brother and he has feelings and he has thoughts just like you and me. Do you think just because he can't turn to that family and say, "Keep staring, I might do a trick," he wouldn't love to say it? Or when he waves to that mom staring at him and she looks back at him and hurries their kids along, do you think that look hurts him? Or when those kids laugh at him and call him a retard, do you think he feels like one? My brother is so much more than some people see. He is a beautiful person. He knows when we are sad, he knows when we are hurt, he knows when we are happy, and he knows when we are serious. So why look at him like he's any less than us?

Down syndrome is often times looked at as a disability. In fact, it is labeled as one. But I don't see it as that. Sometimes I feel like people easily think that people with Down syndrome are something less. They are not less; they are different. Sure, some may not be able to talk, or do simple addition, or live on their own, or have a family. But while us "normal" people (and I use quotes because none of us are normal) may see this as a tragedy, it's not. People with a disability or disorder oftentimes have the most genuine and perfect love that there is. They see the beauty in everything. They can get so excited when they can have a milkshake. They are so joyful when they get a hug from a friend. They can even have a blast and a half with a bungee cord. They see the beauty in both a bright summer day and a rainy day.

I am not saying that having a disability is an easy life. People with disabilities go through enormous amounts of struggle. What I am saying is that we can learn so much from them. They are some of the most incredibly passionate, loving, caring and beautiful people I have ever met and have the privilege to know. So while they may be considered less and labeled as "disabled" because of a tiny chromosome or brain disorder or whatever condition, I say they are more. If we spent more time looking closely, we can find so much to learn from them. We can learn how to appreciate the simple joys of life, how to be happy and thankful for the tiniest things. We can learn how to have fun, enjoy the time that we have, and the things we are given. But most of all, we can learn how to love.

Having a sibling with Down syndrome is tough; I won't lie to you. They will make you angry, they will destroy your homework, crash your parties, and steal your spotlight. But, no matter how much you want to push them over and watch them try to get up like a turtle flipped on its shell, you will always love them at the end of the day. I love my brother. I thank God for him and for the amazing gift he is to my family. I wouldn't change a single thing about him—not even for the all of the birthday wishes in the world.

My Entire Life Changed December 23rd 2003

Written by: Dylan Turner

My entire life changed on December 23, 2003. That day will forever be marked in history for my family, and I will remember it forever. On December 23, my sister Madison was born. When she came into our family for the first time, doctors realized that she had problems with her heart and lungs (pulmonary hypertension). Unlike after my birth, my sister Madison was transferred 50 miles from Los Gatos Community Hospital to Oakland Children's Hospital by helicopter. She stayed at Oakland Children's hospital for one month, and was put on ECMO (A procedure that uses a machine to take over and work for the lungs and heart.) After one month, my little sister came home healthy. I was much too young to remember all our early years of life together, but I can recall what we are experiencing now together.

Madison and I have a basic sibling love-hate relationship. When my friends are over I try to keep her out, and when her friends are over she makes it a point how much she doesn't like me and how I should never come into her room. We may have these little feuds, though we truly do love each other.

One thing my sister loves to do is go to the Embassy Suites in Monterrey. When our family goes there I feel that Madison and I bond more than ever. We love to go down to the lobby extra early in the morning and extra late at night to get food together without our parents. We love to look at the koi fish down there too. While in Monterey, my sister always finds a way of convincing my parents that we should go get ice cream and chocolate at the Ghirardelli store on Cannery Row. One of the most memorable things we do there as siblings is take walks on the beach and make sand castles.

My sister and I call each other buddies for about everything, such as football-buddies, swimming-buddies, or video game-buddies. This is really special to me because I know that Madison will  always have her "sad-buddy" to go to if she is sad about something too, or her "let's play-buddy", when she feels alone. Even though Madison and I like completely different things, we will always have each other.

One thing Madison has taught me is to never judge a book by its cover. If every Average Joe on the street were to see a person with a disability, I guarantee that most of them would think "Oh look at that person over there. I sure do feel sorry for them," though that is definitely not the case.

Many people with disabilities are extremely smart and want to be part of our society like you and I do, such as my sister, Madison. She doesn't want anyone to feel sorry for her at all. At her school, Madison has a huge group of friends and most recesses she is never alone. Madison actually teaches me to be a better person every day. I actually wish I could have the same social skills she has. She is more open, less  self-conscious, and, sadly, much stronger than I am physically. I am not joking; she can really beat me up, LOL.

I really never think of Madison as having Down syndrome at all. Down syndrome is part of our family and part of our life. It makes Madison what she is and I love the person she is.

I love you, my buddy....

The Bond of Sisters

Written by: Elaina Marchenko

It's the beginning of the day; I'm in social studies class. My notebook is on my desk. My teacher needs to run out of the classroom so he asks another teacher to keep an eye on us while he's gone. The other teacher walks in with my sister Polly and another little boy trailing behind her. I get Polly's attention even though everyone is saying "hi" and talking to Polly and the little boy. She comes over and sits with me. ("Is this your homework?") I hug and kiss her and like seeing her away from home. I know my family was concerned with Polly going to my neighborhood school for kindergarten. But I'm glad she goes here.

Most people would think my family is different. I have two younger sisters with special needs. Polly is one of them. Let me be honest, having siblings with special needs isn't always a walk in the park. I think it's more like chasing them through the park. They are just my little sisters, who annoy me and bother me like my other sister Zoya. I get frustrated with their struggle to adapt to different situations. Maybe we can't go do something because it will be too hard for them. It's tiring when I have to help them with things kids usually can do. It's easy to get upset with Polly when she stares at lights or when Evie scratches me or pulls my hair.

But my sisters have taught me some incredible things. Let me tell you about them. I will start with Polly. Polly is seven years old and has Down syndrome. She loves life. The little things that we don't think really count, count in her world. Polly has unconditional love for others. Sometimes my mom is sick and she still wants to be around her and love her anyway. Most people struggle with unconditional love.

Polly says "hi" to everyone. We actually had to teach her not to hug and kiss others at school. She is definitely a social butterfly and is very joyful considering what she went through. When she was three years old she had a seizure and a stroke. She was diagnosed with Moyamoya Syndrome, which means arteries in her brain were too narrow and weren't pumping enough blood. Polly had two brain surgeries to move arteries around so enough blood could be brought to her brain. Even after all that, she still loves to go to the doctor. She tells me to be brave when I'm getting a shot.

Polly has the funniest sense of humor. She enjoys telling jokes even if they don't make sense. "Knock Knock" "Who's there?" She makes a snoring noise then says "a dina-snore!" Polly loves to make herself laugh. And overall she just loves life and I love her.

Now, I would like to talk about my youngest sister. Evangeline is my other sister with special needs. Evie is six months younger than Polly and has Down syndrome and autism. She also has a very sweet heart. We adopted her from the Ukraine in 2009. It has been four years since we adopted her and she is finally reaching out to us. Getting to know her is thrilling. Sometimes autism can make it hard for her to connect. Therefore, when you feel a connection with her it's gratifying. Evie has taken a while to show her personality; her likes and dislikes. Evie likes music and going places, lettuce-y type foods, and light-up toys. She doesn't like being cooped up at home. Evie is non-verbal but she uses pictures and objects to communicate. For her to communicate with us is a lot of progress considering how distant she was a few years ago, closer to when we first adopted her.

You can tell Evie is Ukrainian because of the traditional food she enjoys; like soups, meat, and potatoes. She enjoys going to school and rough housing. She's very ticklish. Her laugh is adorable. She's my buddy. You have to keep an eye on Evie because if you don't, she can swipe food or knock over drinks when you aren't looking. We call her a ninja because of how fast she can take crayons at church or cause a mess. She also gets into mischief with our dog, Scout.

I remember the day Evie came home from the orphanage. We were in Ukraine at my grandma's small apartment. It was awkward because we weren't great at playing together yet. I was sitting on the floor worried that when she rocked on the couch she would dive off. Now, playing with each other feels natural and there isn't a barrier between us. She is my sister no matter what. That won't change.

Even though our family is different, special needs have positively affected our family. There is a lot of good that has come from having sisters with special needs. We were introduced to the special needs community where there are so many people who understand our family and have good solutions to problems we share. We also go to Gigi's Playhouse, a place where we attend open-plays; a time where families with kids who have Down syndrome and their siblings come and play with others. We connect with other families, meet new kids, and help reach out to families affected by special needs. I've met a lot of other kids with Down syndrome who are full of joy like Polly and Evie.

When it comes down to it, Polly and Evie are simply my sisters. That's it. Having an extra chromosome is pretty cool. That's one more than I have. Most people only have 46 chromosomes whereas, people with Down syndrome have 47. I know Down syndrome is different, I get it. But God has a plan for my sisters just like he has one for me and everybody else. My sisters have changed my life. When you meet people with special needs, take a minute to get to know them. It will change your perspective on life. I wouldn't be who I am today without them.

The Greatest of These is Love

Written by: Tucker Goulding

This is not my story but, Charity and Neko's story. Charity and Neko are (I am going to just say it) the most amazing people I have ever meet. They both have what you call Down syndrome but, since I don't like saying it (no offense to John Iagen Down), I am just going to call it love syndrome. Sure they have their moments and aren't always obedient but, they sure make up for it. I think God made people like Charity and Neko with a specific purpose in life that no other person can fill. God made them extra special and not by just adding an extra chromosome but, he added extra life, joy, forgiveness, happiness, love, and the list goes on. These people are not your everyday people they are the ones who do what you think is crazy like hugging a teenage boy walking back from school who they don't even know or touching the arm of a homeless woman and saying hello. There is something about these people that, when doing these things, LOVE flows out from them.

When we first adopted Charity into our family she was the

cutest baby I had ever seen. The saddest thing to me was that no one wanted her and she would have been sent to the state to be put into foster home after foster home. Now I am not saying foster homes are bad but, this is not what God had planned for her and looking back she might not have lived if she was put up by the state. Once at our home she was doing great until one day when she was 7 weeks old she stopped breathing. I was scared because I didn't want her to die. After that she has been to the hospital numerous times, had many surgeries, almost died more then once. She has had kidney infections, a small trachea, and other problems. Through out this whole time I was scared, sad, and even cried. I am very happy that Charity is here today. She is the very miracle of life. Each day is a gift filled with life from God.

Through the whole process with Charity in the hospital, my mom and dad were considering adopting again. This thought became a reality when we brought home Neko on  November 2nd. Neko has not had as much medical problems as Charity, but having 2 children with LOVE syndrome has it's challenges. Neko has been our social boy who is always making new friends. The reason he makes friends is he is fun to be around and is always making you laugh. Neko is such a joy to have in our family and every day he shows all of us what happens when you live in the moment.

So if you were to ask me if my life with Charity and Neko was everything I thought it would be, I would say no, it is BETTER. Charity and Neko have taught me so much about living that I can truly say I would not be the same person I am today without them in my life. When we first had Charity and Neko in our home I was always embarrassed when we went out in public. This is because our family is not your average family. For one thing we have six children; for another we have two children with love syndrome. I used to be always embarrassed because we did not fit into society but, then it dawned on me, society doesn't want these children anyway so why do I want to fit into society? The answer was because I didn't care about Charity and Neko but, I cared about myself. I have now learned that this is the worst way to live your life. Charity and Neko have taught me how to be patient, kind, and how to love without being loved back. It is all about others in this life and if you only care about yourself then you are missing out on the world. So I am proud to say that I have 2 siblings with LOVE syndrome.

"faith, hope, and love but, the greatest of these is Love." Jesus

Beauty Exposed

Adult Siblings

The following stories are written by adults who have grown up with, and know what it is like to live with and love their siblings with Down syndrome.

"What I noticed about growing up with Charlie is that, he would see the little things and be so excited! Also, he loves everybody. We all helped Charlie be included in all our activities, treated him as normal." Looking back she said, "it helped me choose good friends because of how people responded to Charlie."

Emily Baer

"It is no different then living with any other sibling, it is what it is. It is what you make it."

Steve Stafford

Beauty Exposed

My Brother Bobby

Written by: Dwayne Breese

My name is Dwayne, and my brother is Bobby. He has Down syndrome. Bobby was 61 years old in 2013. I have always looked up to my brother, as he was older than I, and bigger until I got taller than him. I would tease him and say I was the bigger brother; he would say, "I am older".

All my life he has been my brother, friend, confidant, and I was the same for him, except for when I got older. Then I was his protector as well. I protected him from others that would make fun of him when we went shopping or on outings.

First and foremost are the things we used to do together. Playing in the dirt, the backyard, swinging, riding pedal cars, and tricycles, and splashing in the kiddie pool. Taking care of the pets we had--cats, dogs, guinea pigs and ducks.

These and more memories came back recently as I had 8mm home films transferred to DVD for easier viewing. We had not seen these movies in so many years. It was an exciting day when I got these back. I told Bobby about watching them and he said, "OK". Oh, my, he was giddy watching it and laughing along with me as we remembered all the things we saw. We saw Christmases past where Santa stopped by on Christmas Eve and gave us our presents. Dad was a fireman with the local fire station. One of the crew would put on his Santa suit and visit other kids in the area, and he stopped at our house. We saw the camping trips we took, splashing in creeks and rivers, sleeping in tents, along with fishing.

Mealtime was always fun with Bobby. He would set the plates on the table and wait for dinner, as he was "Born Hungry", he would say. Afterwards, he would set about collecting the plates and washing the dishes. He was always prompt, and if things didn't go on schedule he would get "grumpy" because things had to be on time. I think he got that from Mom, as she was the one that made sure we all were on time and early for appointments.

He has his jobs around the house, like collecting the mail, getting the paper in the morning, reading the TV Guide when it comes in the mail. Surprising to us was his recognition of words and times in the TV Guide. Right after the guide came, he would take it in his room and go through it page by page. When he was done he would come and tell us what program was on (if it was different from the regularly scheduled one). We would look and be astounded by his remarkable memory and how he could retain that bit of entertainment to tell us when it would be on.

Bobby has always had good health, with which we have been blessed.

It is sad watching your brother get old and grey as I am also. But, then again, I am elated that he has the opportunity to do so. To have a brother all these years means so much to me. He taught me so much in his ability to smile at things that others don't see. I would not be the person I am today without my older brother Bobby and my parents as they raised us with the aspect that there is no disability that cannot be conquered. Here's to my brother Bobby.

Jason

Written by: Jenni Ross

I don't remember life before Jason was born. I imagine I enjoyed my two years as an only child, but I simply have no recollection of life without him. The memories I do have include: pulling Jason across our tile floor to hear him giggle, sitting together on the couch as we went on an imaginary trip with my dolls, and running alongside him the very first time he rode a two-wheel bicycle. There are other memories as well: visiting doctor's offices, watching therapists come in and out of our house, and constantly translating Jason's developing speech to others. The memories meld together, not one more specific than another, not one less "normal" than another.

The first time I remember defining Down syndrome was when my parents and I gave a presentation to Jason's fourth grade class. We knew his peers were asking questions and felt if we could explain some details, they would be more accepting as they  got older. They were, at times – but not always. As a big sister I defended my brother when others took advantage of him or teased him. Many times Jason didn't even notice, but I felt it was my responsibility to guard his dignity.

As we grew up, I worked to create new ways for Jason to be included. In high school I created a club that hosted social opportunities for students with and without disabilities. I co-founded PALS Programs, which began as a weeklong sleep away camp for young adults with Down syndrome. In college, I founded Princeton Disability Awareness and hosted an annual Down Syndrome Conference for children with Down syndrome, their siblings and families. Through each of these programs, I worked to bring others into the world where I lived, and provide them with the experience of knowing someone with Down syndrome.

For many who have never met someone with Down syndrome, it might be difficult to imagine how much can be gained from someone with a disability, someone who–by society's standards–is lacking. People with Down syndrome are burdened by many stereotypes–most degrading, if not offensive. None of them come to mind when I think of Jason. Through Jason, I have learned what it means to be strong, courageous, sincere, and honest. Jason has shown me how to forgive others, how to experience joy in the smallest of moments, and how to love radically.

After graduating Princeton, I found a new home working for Special Olympics. Their mission challenges and inspires me every day, but the real honor is working for an organization that has directly enhanced Jason's life. Beyond sport, which has provided Jason with many opportunities, Special Olympics has taught him about advocacy.

Over the past two years, Jason has developed a new hero–

his name is Tim Shriver. Although not completely lacking in superhuman powers, Tim became Jason's hero for a simple reason: he gave Jason a voice. When Jason spoke, Tim listened. When Jason attended a meeting, Tim asked for his insight. When Jason was by himself, Tim joined him.

Through this simple acceptance, these acts of inclusion, and this demonstration that he valued Jason, Tim transformed Jason's world and empowered him to begin reaching his full potential. Tim represents only a small example of the power that a movement like Special Olympics brings with it. A power that, to no one's surprise, started with the passion and determination of a sibling.

So why does this matter? As a sibling of someone with Down syndrome, the question I am asked most often is the following: Would you change it if you could? If you could separate Jason from his diagnosis of Down syndrome, would you take away the disability?

Looking back, I consider the many ways I've worked to make Jason included, to have people see his value. The common theme is that I've never once considered changing Jason. I try to give others new experiences, transform people's misconceptions and redirect their expectations. Like a recent Special Olympics advertisement I read, my goal has been to make others rethink, to consider "truth without judgment, love without boundaries, and respect without requirements." If I am eliminating a disability, the disability is not in Jason—it's in the world.

So what is it like to have a sibling with Down syndrome? It is an honor. Jason's life is nothing short of a gift, and his presence in mine is one of God's greatest blessings.

The Floyd Sisters

Written by: Kelly Floyd

Having a sibling with Down syndrome has been one of the most amazing experiences for me. When my little sister, Kaitlyn, was born in 2004, I was a 13 year-old who had been an only child my entire life, so not only did my world change because I had a sibling, it also changed because my new sister was special. Now, nine years later I am 22 years old and married, but no one has impacted my life more than she has. I did not realize then exactly how special Kaitlyn truly is.

The months after she was born are mostly a blur, but there are a few moments that are etched in my memory. The first moment was when the doctors came in and told us that they believed she had Down syndrome. I remember being in shock and seeing my parents crying, then beginning to cry myself. I was not crying because I didn't have a perfectly healthy sister, I was not crying because I was sad, I was crying because I was afraid. In that moment I was so afraid for my sister and the struggles she was going to face for her entire life, I would have done anything to make her not have Down syndrome. The second moment was when they had to transport her by helicopter to the closest major hospital because she had three holes in her heart, could not take a bottle, and other various reasons. I remember seeing her in this incubator with so many things stuck in her or stuck to her getting ready to make the trip and thinking that my sister was going to die. I remember the long drive to the hospital they brought her to and the complete silence that took over the vehicle. We were all so scared. The third moment I remember was Kaitlyn's open heart surgery. I was not there the day of the surgery, but my parents were there and I was at home with my grandmothers. I remember not being able to focus on anything or sit still all day long waiting for the news that my sister had made it through surgery. When I was finally able to go to the hospital and see my sister, I remember looking at her as if it was not real. She was so swollen and had so many tubes going into various places of her body, she looked like some kind of machine. I was so afraid she was going to die that I couldn't even be in the

room for too long because I did not want to be there when she died. I hated that hospital room, I hated being in that hospital.

After my sister recovered from her open heart surgery and became strong enough to eat on her own to have her feeding tube removed, I became secure in knowing that my sister would not only survive but that she would also succeed because she was a fighter. In the eight and a half years since that moment, my sister has taught me so many things. She has taught me to never give up, to smile in the face of adversity, and that a good attitude can get you anywhere. She is the most genuine and loving person I have ever, and will ever, meet. She makes me laugh when she knows I am upset, she makes me smile when she knows I have had a bad day, and, most importantly, she shows me love when I feel like there is no love left to give. I treasure her more than anything in this world because, what she does not understand, is that at one point nine years ago I never thought I would be here with her today. I never thought that my sister with Down syndrome would not only be my best friend but also the one person who I could never live without. I thought that I would be the one who would have to protect her, and who knows maybe one day I will, but to this day she has been the one who I go to when I need support, even if all she can do is hug me, tell me it's okay, and then make me laugh so hard I forget what I was upset about in the first place.

There are so many moments that I have looked at my sister and realized that I do not even see her as a child with Down syndrome, I see her as a normal kid, because she really is. She goes to school, does gymnastics, goes to dance class, made her first communion, and, most importantly, she dreams big. I know I never have to worry about what will become of her because I know she will not settle for anything less then what she wants for herself. She makes me not settle for anything less then what I want for myself. She is my role model and, if given the chance now, I would never trade having a sister with Down syndrome for having a sister without.

What is Love?

Written by: Marianne Marts

Love, what does it look like?

Giving a tight neck-kinking hug, silly faces, head rubs, family time and McDonalds gift cards, to just name a few. Who is Joey? Joey is a fun loving enthusiastic guy who loves pretty girls, his family and co-workers at the barber shop. He enjoys watching old TV shows, listening to Billy Joel, Kenny Rodgers, creating his calendars and tap dancing and, oh, he happens to have Down syndrome.

As an adult sib of an aging adult with Down syndrome, I have recently reflected on some things from my childhood with great emotion. I just recently found out that, out of my six siblings, I was the only one who ever grew up with Joey at home with me my entire life. With Joey being 14 years older and me being the youngest and only girl, my role is extremely unique. Even though I am the youngest, I carry older kids' tendencies, especially since I am his guardian. It is because of Joey that I became a teacher, professional advocate, trainer, author and national speaker. He has helped shape me, my thinking and my desires. I remember that, when growing up, he would hug me so tight that I would get neck kinks and it took a long time to teach him to be gentle. But he did. I also remember the opposite, where he would kick or punch holes in the walls.   Due to his violent & self-abusive behaviors I shied away from having friends over.

During my brother's 54th birthday party I ran into an old neighbor /school friend who lived across the alley from us. When we were talking I

© www.joeysupswithdowns.com / www.facebook.com/joeysups
Teaching we are more alike than different.

asked if he remembered Joey and he said no, which then made me sink inside. About three weeks later I began to contemplate why he didn't know/remember Joey. I don't remember much earlier than middle school myself. I never knew how to explain Joey to them. I really didn't understand what he had, just that he was different and had behaviors I couldn't explain. Only when I was in high school did I do a paper on Down syndrome and begin to gain a better understanding myself.

A few years later, we unexpectedly lost our father. I was only 15 and my role quickly and dramatically changed in regards to Joey. I no longer was a younger sib but now became a parent. The day our father passed, I was actually upset with him and Joey, as I was forced to take him around the fair. I was 15 and I didn't want my sib hanging around with me. Once I accepted this role change, it also altered my life journey. After college I willingly became one of Joey's co-guardians along with my mom and another brother. It was at that point that I had made two decisions. One, that whomever I marry has to love Joey as much as I do (This one was part of my prayer list for my hubby). I urge you not to settle, it is not worth it. I waited until I was 33 to marry, because finding the one God had for me was important not just for me but for Joey as well. Two, I chose not to have kids so that I would be able to advocate effectively for him and my mom as she ages. When my

husband, Karl, met Joey the first time as we were dating, he brought Joey a hand carved heart airbrushed "Jesus loves Joey". I was in tears. Now Karl has the most amazing  relationship with Joey, more than I could have ever asked or prayed for.

We have begun a new journey with the three of us. The last 2 years he has slowed down and mellowed in behaviors. I enjoy that he is more easily re-directed but it does come with costs of physical and mental drawbacks of remaining active. It is hard to watch as it determines what is ahead. I know that his life has been full of lots of great and new experiences. Especially these last 18 months, since the children's book I wrote about him was published: <u>Will YOU Be My Friend</u>?- the first book in the "Joey's Ups with Downs" children's series. (www.joeysupswithdowns.com / www.facebook.com/joeysups). I am able to have Joey join us at local book signings and events and he is in his element.   I know that by my involvement in his life it has only made him better and vice versa. I would have life no other way.

Joey has taught me more than any degree I have or could earn. He is with me wherever I go, in what I say, or how I treat people. My hubby and I quote Joeyisms all the time like "oooh boy", or "I had fun", or "mooooove" with the gestures of course! So in honor of Joey - "I had fun!" So what is love - it is Joey!

www.joeysupswithdowns.com

Janice Kristina

Written by: Stephanie Turner

Janice Kristina was born on June 9, 1985. My mother was a mere 25 years old, giving birth to her second child. She had no idea that this 6 pound infant had an abnormality that had been stitched deep into her DNA at the moment of conception. My mother did everything right, she took care of herself. She was young. And yet her infant was diagnosed with Down syndrome shortly after birth. I was 11 months and 14 days old when Janice was born, so I do not remember those early days, and I cannot comment on how my parents coped with her diagnosis. I can, however, tell you how I coped and what my earliest memories of her were.

I remember a smiley face with big blue eyes and blond hair. I remember her infectious giggle. I remember a 3 year old wobbly Janice learning to walk and all of us clapping with joy. I remember learning I could get over on my little sister. If I stood on the tippy top of my toes I could stretch my chubby little arm in between the bars on her crib and grab her bottle and enjoy the milk that was inside. I was eventually found out and reprimanded. I remember when

Janice got her first big girl bed and I just HAD to sleep in it with her, you know, so she wouldn't get scared.

As we aged, our developmental gap widened. It was about 1st grade when I became embarrassed of Janice. I was a painfully shy child and wanted nothing more than to be accepted, and kids can be cruel. I don't like talking about this, but I want to be real. I purposely avoided Janice if we came into contact at school. I looked away. I tried to steer conversation away from "the special class." If I had been a more confident child, maybe I would have run to her, hugged her, told everyone that she was my sister, and that she looks a bit different, but she's not much different than you and I. But I didn't do that. This general way of thinking and behaving went on until middle school when we actually had the same gym period. The counselor offered to move me to a different class, but I refused. Maybe I subconsciously wanted to watch over her, but I kept her relation to me a secret. Somehow, a group of mean girls found out and straight up asked me if she was my sister. I should have said, yes she is! So what? I should have told them I was proud of her, but I didn't. I lied. I told them she wasn't my sister and to this day it pains me that I couldn't be stronger and tell the truth.

When I got to high school my confidence came. I had a close group of friends who knew Janice and loved her. I even volunteered to help when Janice's class traveled to the Special Olympics for the day. I still got frustrated with her, just like any other sibling, but I wasn't ashamed anymore. This was my normal and it was ok. I had come to terms with Janice and I loved her. She bugged me sometimes, but I loved her.

When I got married in 2007, Janice was my bell ringer. The look of pride on her face as she walked down that aisle will stay with me always. I am her idol. Janice thinks the sun rises and sets with me, and I could never convince her that I am not worthy of such praise, so I will try to make her proud instead. Janice is stubborn, she is sweet, she is incredibly witty and she loves to indulge in culinary delights. She loves playing with transformers and she loves Disney Princesses. Janice can read and write and loves to draw. Janice does not see color, nor does she judge. She is everything I wish I was. She lives life to the fullest and loves without abandon. I was recently crowned Mrs. Tennessee International and I needed to choose a platform that would be close to my heart. Janice is 28 now. I didn't even have to think about it. I knew I wanted to advocate for adults with intellectual disabilities. I am now busy advocating and doing what I can to inform others that adults with disabilities deserve an education, and to be accepted and included in their

communities. Janice has taught me compassion. Janice has taught me patience. Janice has taught me not to fear differences. Janice has taught me that the most important things in life don't cost money or make us beautiful. Janice has taught me more than I could have ever learned in

school. The most important thing is how you treat others, and how you live your life to the fullest, despite limitations. Growing up with Janice has made me who I am today. When I see someone struggling I don't look away. I don't keep going. I offer help. I am not afraid of differences, I embrace them.

Growing up with Janice was not always easy for me, but those shortcomings were my own, not hers, and just like many young people, I had to find myself to see the light. I am utterly grateful I grew up with Janice as my sister and I wouldn't change her for the world. I will continue to use my crown to make her proud, and I will continue to advocate and try to make a difference in the lives of others with intellectual disabilities.

My Little Sister

Written by: Cheryl Pavitt

I was 5 years old when Laurie was born on June 15, 1970. I remember the day that my mother brought her home from the hospital like it was yesterday. Laurie was like my little doll that I used to play with and at one point, I remember picking her up and the next thing I knew she was on the floor. I remember that she laid there looking at me for a minute and then she started screaming. My mother ran in to see what had happened and that was a story that we talked about for years to come. Laurie loved telling people that her older sister Cheryl dropped her on her head.

Laurie was born with a congenital heart defect. Laurie was in and out of the hospital for most of her childhood with pneumonia. It was difficult being 5 years old and going from always having my mom to myself to my mom being at the hospital all the time with her. I never knew who was going to be picking me up from school and then I would spend the rest of the evening sitting at the hospital until it was time to go home. Laurie was always sick and having to go to the doctor's all the time. Unfortunately, when she was born, they were not doing heart surgeries to fix the holes in her heart like they do today when children are born with these heart defects. They told us in the beginning that she wouldn't live to be 2 and then it was 18 because of her heart defect. Laurie was one of the strongest people I had ever met and she defied all the odds. Laurie lived to be 41 years old and passed away on January 4, 2012. I being the oldest sister, decided that I had to be the one that delivered her Eulogy and it was the most difficult thing I had ever done. It was heart wrenching, but also heartwarming as it forced me to remember who she was and what she truly meant to me, to everyone.

She was the nucleus of our family that kept us together and brought us together. Even though I lived 3,000 miles away for a good portion of her life, I called her every day and saw her at least once a year. Our phone calls were the highlights of my day. I would call her on my way home from work and she would fill me in on her daily events along with what was happening within the family. Her sense of humor would make me laugh and I miss those daily phone calls along with the great big hugs that only she could give to me.

Laurie moved into a group home when she was 30. She had a roommate and they had staff there 24 hours a day. Laurie loved living on her own and having her independence. She had her own birthday parties at her house and also hosted a yearly Halloween party where she would invite all of her family and friends. She would get so excited to have everyone over to her house. Laurie loved her niece Ashley and her nephew Jacob. Laurie was very close to Ashley, and Ashley used to help her take showers when she stayed at my mom's house for the holidays.

I never realized the impact that she had on my life until I had gotten older and then I couldn't ever imagine life without her. Coming to terms with that has been the most difficult obstacle for me to overcome in my life. I will never, ever forget her and she gave me so much more than even she knew.

Even in death, she is still giving me blessings. Laurie passed away on January 4, 2012 and I was blessed with a granddaughter, Isabella on March 12, 2012 who also has Down syndrome. I truly believe that Laurie sent her to me knowing that is what I needed. Bella has a t-shirt that says, "My Grandma made a wish and I came true." How fitting is that.

Below is the Eulogy that I wrote for Laurie's funeral. This summarizes how much she meant to me, her family and all of her friends. It is difficult to capture all of the memories that I have of Laurie into words because there are so many wonderful memories to share. I frequently go to the cemetery to reflect and think about all of the wonderful memories that I'm blessed to have.

Laurie's Eulogy

Laurie truly was a gift from God who brought so much joy to her family and all of her friends. She was our angel here on earth and is now our angel in heaven.

Family and friends were extremely important to her and she loved to have everyone over to her house. She hosted her own birthday parties and had an annual Halloween party that no one ever dressed up for including her. It didn't matter what the party was for, but just having everyone together was everything to her and she was always so proud to have us over to her home.

She loved living on her own, her Barbie doll, going to the casino, going to the mall for her weekly blueberry muffin with a soda, going out to eat and oh, how she loved her weekly Dairy Queen blizzards with chocolate ice cream and M&M's. Her favorite thing to do was watch DVD's and she would get fixated for long periods of time on one particular DVD that she watched every single night. I would say to her, "What DVD are you watching tonight and she would giggle and say, You know." It was always either Karate Kid with Jackie Chan or Selena. Sometimes, these 2 movies would "mysteriously" disappear for a period of time and I always knew when the staff at Blackstone had enough of watching them. She was extremely intelligent, loving, loyal, set in her ways, loved taking her showers and our phone calls would consist of her mentioning the nightly shower every single day. She was notorious for trying to pull a "fast one." She recently called to tell me that she had not gotten her weekly blizzard and had this detailed "story" about why she had not gotten it. So the next time I saw her, I took her to Dairy Queen to get one. I asked her what size she wanted and she wasn't sure so I told her to go big or go home. She brought home a large and the staff informed me that she did have a blizzard that week. I couldn't believe that she had pulled one over on me and that I fell for it.

Laurie provided us all with many gifts including compassion, generosity, forgiveness, independence, sensitivity, strength, a sense of humor even up until the very end and a will to live like no other. She inspired me to be the best person I can be. She lived life to the absolute fullest and on her own terms. She was able to do and see things that most of us have never had the chance to see or accomplish. She overcame obstacles every day and did it with determination, love, and pride. One of the greatest gifts that she taught and gave to all of us was her unconditional love. She was a role model for us all and we should each strive to keep her memory alive by telling everyone how much we love them every day just like she did.

Laurie, now you no longer have to miss daddy because you are now in his loving arms. I'd like to thank my Mom and Stepdad for taking such good care of her all these years, and Dad, please take care of my little sister. I am sad for all of the tomorrows in which she will not be an active participant, but that sadness is tempered with the belief that we will all be together again. That she is right now with her dad, making plans for the day that they will greet each of us with a smile and a hug.

I look forward to that day, but for now will be satisfied with the many wonderful memories that I have of the most loving, caring person that I have ever known.

Our family will never be the same without her, but we were blessed to have her in our lives for so many wonderful years. Laurie, it is an honor to be your sister and to be loved by you. Rest in peace, my little sister, and as we always ended our telephone conversations, "I love you, I miss you and I'll see you soon."

Life in the Fast Lane

Written by: David Ragan

My name is David Ragan and my older brother, Adam Ragan, has Down syndrome. He is a couple years older than I am, and is a big supporter of my racing career. Living with a brother that has Down syndrome teaches you that you can overcome any obstacle life throws at you, if you give it your all. Adam has a lot of challenges every day that I don't have to face. He tackles them like anyone else does, and moves on to the next task. He works at David Ragan Ford in Perry, Georgia. He helps the sales team with all the customers, cleans the facility, and answers phones whenever he can. Adam truly shows that working hard and never giving up, can lead to achieving any goal.

Please visit **www.dsrtfraceforresearch.org** to learn about the 'Race for Research' David is doing to raise awareness about Down syndrome.

My Younger Sister Sharlene

Written by: Dawn Gaunt-Cooke

My younger sister, Sharlene (we call her Sissy), had Down syndrome. She passed away on February 3, 2013 of Early Onset Alzheimers. She was 51. She was a twin to my sister Terrilyn, who doesn't have Down syndrome. All three of us were the same age for 9 days. Back in the 1960's doctors and specialists suggested institutionalizing children born with disabilities. My mom would not have it. She was a single mother and that would have been the easy way for her. She raised Sissy the same way she raised me and her twin Terrilyn. We took dance lessons and Sissy took dance lessons. She went to church and catechism with us. Sissy loved to dance and I know she is dancing in heaven now.

Sissy attended Special Education classes in public school. Special Education was a lot different in the 70's. The classes were mostly in basements of the school and they were kept separate from the rest of the students. It was there that she met her best friend, Rosie, and her boyfriend, Jerry. Rosie also had Down syndrome. They had sleep overs and participated in Special Olympics together, dances and various other activities. Sissy and Jerry would talk on the phone every day. They wanted to get married but not have a baby because, as she would say, "I don't want to get fat." She didn't have the patience for little kids. She also wanted to

drive. We used to tell her that her feet had to get bigger so she could drive. She was always waiting for her feet to grow. It probably wasn't nice to tell her that but it seemed to satisfy her.

Our mom had to work several jobs to support us. I was the oldest so I took on the caretaking role. A lot of the time, if I wanted to go out with my friends, I had to take her with me. I resented it at the time. She would tell on me that I was smoking or with boys, or at parties.

After she aged out of school, she went to "Sunshine Village", a sheltered workshop of sorts. She hated it there but eventually got a job as a dishwasher at Al's Diner, where she worked until the Alzheimer's prevented her from doing her job. She made lots of friends there. She liked to cash her check and buy wine coolers or beer. One day my mom came home and found that Sissy drank ½ a bottle of her wine and was a bit tipsy.

Sissy loved music and dancing. She had a disco ball in her room. She wanted long blond hair like Brittney Spears. She liked Fonzie and The Hulk. My mom was an animal lover and we had lots of animals over the years. Some she liked some sissy didn't. She could be heard saying "stupid cat," or other colorful words. I don't know why, but certain animals she would develop a bond with. The one I remember the most was a Greyhound named Happy Dog.

When I started my own family she would come and stay at my house. She didn't like it as much as she liked being with her own stuff, and I liked everything in its place and I wouldn't let her stay on the phone for hours with Jerry. I also would always cut her fingernails, which she hated.

I started noticing maybe 6 or 7 years ago that she was getting very forgetful and couldn't write as well. She loved writing notes and "I Love Jerry." My mom didn't notice it at first as she was closer to it. She got to the point where she couldn't stay alone anymore and would, at times, get aggressive. She didn't remember Jerry anymore as time went on. Over the next 5 years she became a shell of who she was. A pit bull my mom owned had bonded with her and always slept with her. I believe that dog gave her comfort and took away some of the pain. We could still get her to laugh almost right up until the end. She was very attached to my mom and her boyfriend. She used to say baby, baby, baby, which turned into B, B, B as she couldn't talk anymore. Soon she didn't eat anymore and her body grew tired. On February 3rd 2013 she became an angel in Heaven.

My sister taught me that everyone has value and every human can do "stuff" and everyone deserves respect and love. Maybe that's why God puts people with Downs on the earth to teach us that.

My Brother Das

Written by: Dr. Kishore Vellody

My brother, Das, and I were always "the boys" when we were growing up. We were inseparable. His friends were my friends, and my friends were his friends. However, our personalities were so different! Looking back through our childhood pictures, one cannot help but notice his goofy smiles and my "about to cry" face in nearly every picture. Yet, despite our different personalities, we were always together. To this day, we continue to have a bond unlike any other "typical" sibling pair I have ever met.

Das has always had to work so hard to learn new things. I remember many occasions trying to teach him something, but he just couldn't seem to "get it" as quickly as I thought he should! I would get so frustrated, but my parents would always encourage me to slow down to learn what Das was actually teaching me – patience! Over time, I recognized that sometimes it takes a struggle to see what it means to truly celebrate a victory. Das taught me the value of hard work, and he inspired me to finally "apply myself" in school. That determination saw me all the way through my medical training, and, eventually into my career choice as a pediatrician.

In 2009, just a handful of years into my career as a

pediatrician at Children's Hospital of Pittsburgh, my life took a whole new direction. The hospital was looking for someone to take over the Down Syndrome Center at the hospital. This Center was previously directed by a legend in the field who unexpectedly passed away. Despite stepping into some very big shoes, I did not feel anxious as I moved forward into the new position. After all, Das had been training me for this my whole life.

Now, I spend so many of my days indirectly giving back to my brother by helping children with Down syndrome achieve their full potential. Most importantly, I work with their families and with their siblings to encourage them to  listen to what their family member with Down syndrome is teaching them. They are teaching them that life is not about IQs, and it's not about SAT scores or college exams. It's not even about being "successful" in a high paying job. My brother has shown everyone that he has ever met that a loving smile and a hug are worth more than any of those things. Diplomas and paychecks will all fade away into nothing, but love endures forever. It's something I'm so grateful that Das continues to teach all of us to this day.

An Extra Dose of Love:
A Brother's Story of Trisomy 21

Written by: Isaac Latterell

My youngest sister, Eva, just turned 12 this past December 31st. Each year, my parents invite friends and family over to celebrate the New Year and the birth of our favorite family member at our New Year's "Eva" party. Now I know, we aren't supposed to have favorites, and our large family would seem to make unanimous consent impossible.

Maybe it's because she's the baby of the family. But there is something special about Eva, qualities she possesses that I believe truly make her a superior human being. First, she has an extra dose of adorable, that magical quality that melts frowns and lights up the faces of the grumpiest strangers. Second, she possesses an effervescent life and joy that I, with all my striving, have never been able to attain.

But most importantly, Eva is blessed with anf extra helping of Love. Eager to shower you with affection and quick to forgive, she exemplifies 1 Corinthians 13:5 which says that love keeps no record of wrongs. Sometimes, I think she must realize her superiority, because she also has an extra pinch of stubbornness. Just calling it intensity would be too generous, but either way, it just makes for never ending jokes, playful sarcasm, and fun!

Scripture teaches us that Love is the most important, indispensable quality of them all. What good are my talents, my wisdom, my wealth, and my generosity, if I don't have love? Isn't this what we are all striving for? I used to think I was pretty smart. But life has a way of showing us how the things we take pride in are useless when we do not have love–when we don't accept God's love for us, and in turn, love others as ourselves.

It was actually another sister, Grace, who helped me realize this first. Grace, now 24 years old, has the same extra dose of love, joy, adorability, and an indomitable spirit like Eva. One time, Grace started driving the riding lawn mower down the street because she wanted to go to the mall.

When I was struggling to get my focus off of myself, enjoy life, and love others, watching Grace and Eva enjoy life and love others instead of being self-absorbed taught me to redefine my concept of intelligence. If the greatest of these is love, how could I say that I am smarter than Grace? Is she not happier, more loving? Is she not more intelligent, and dare I say, superior?

I feel incredibly lucky and blessed to have not one, but two superior human beings that I can call my sister. And I am sad, incredibly sad, that so few people have the opportunity to know a friend like Grace and Eva, let alone the privilege of having one in their family.

You see, 75-90% of children with these magical qualities do not survive until their birth day. But it's not because of any life threatening condition or complication with the pregnancy. It's because when their parents discovered they were about to give birth to a superior human being, they made the tragic and legal decision to terminate their child's life.

Where do these children get their extra dosage of love? I believe it is contained in their DNA. Instead of the 46 chromosomes of DNA that most people have, Grace and Eva have 47. The scientific name for it is Trisomy 21.

Yes, these parents were likely misinformed as to the meaning of this extra DNA, and instead of judging them, I know that there is forgiveness offered by Jesus, who prayed even for his own captors "Father, forgive them, for they know not what they do."

That's why I am writing this article, to help you see what a treasure my sisters are, and how much they can teach us about what is truly important in life. We must not allow our jealousy of these children's superiority to cause us to discriminate, and put them down before they even have the chance to shower their love on us.

That is also why I am introducing the Down syndrome and Genetic Abnormality Non-Discrimination Act. The common name for Trisomy 21 is Down syndrome, and even superior children have the right to enjoy their first birthday, to blow out their candles, and to drive lawn tractors down the street. Please join me in ending discrimination and support equal rights for pre-born people with superior abilities.

Stephen and Lila

Written by: Emily Nowak

When I was two years old, I received the news that excites and dismays young children around the world: you're going to be a big sister.

I was thrilled. Mom got me a baby doll that was almost as big as me and I named him Stanley and dotingly took care of him. I was going to be the best sister ever—just like my older sister was to me.

When Stephen was finally born, I never realized things weren't normal. I didn't know his heart was failing. I didn't know babies weren't normally blue. I didn't know his eyes and nose and fingers were shaped funny. I didn't know he would have trouble talking or that he wouldn't ever "catch up". I didn't know that 90% of other mothers now would have aborted him. I just proclaimed, "He's amazing" and Stephen and I became best buddies for the next few years.

Soon another brother joined our family, also with special needs. He passed away right before his first birthday, and Stephen and I were even closer while Mom and Dad and big sister were grieving.

As time passed, I caught on to the differences between Stephen and other kids his age. When our sister, Lila, was born when I was 7 and Stephen was 5, I was fully aware that as different as life had been with one child in the family with Down syndrome, two was going to be crazy.

It was a good kind of crazy, but sometimes it was a bad kind of crazy. It isn't easy being the sibling of special needs siblings. As our family continued to grow, my typical siblings and I sometimes felt as if Stephen and Lila were the focal point of our family. Sometimes we were excluded by our "friends" or told hurtful things by well-meaning people. Sometimes they felt like just too much to handle.

But they never really were too much to handle. Instead, they have shaped our family and made us all better people. They taught us compassion and sensitivity and how to love unconditionally and how to have fun and even how to clean up 5 pounds of flour on a soaking wet child and how to get stuck donuts out of the VCR. As I got older, I began volunteering with Special Olympics and other special needs organizations, and when I went to college, I became a home aide for special needs families and shaped my courses to reflect my love for special education. I also became actively involved in the pro-life movement. I can say none of these would have happened if it weren't for the influence of Stephen and Lila on our family.

Now Stephen is about to turn 21, and Lila is 16. Stephen is a "businessman" (bagging groceries at the store part time), a football fanatic, a Scooby-Doo enthusiast and the kindest most thoughtful boy I know. He calls me regularly to leave sweet messages on my phone; "I love you, Emily and I'm taking you on a date out to dinner." Lila truly believes she is a cowgirl and never takes off her ragged old vest and hat. She will be my maid of honor in my wedding in a few months and is the most creative young lady—spending hours writing stories about the Wild West and Clara Barton.

When Stephen was born we had no idea what we were getting into. Now we wouldn't change it for the world. It breaks my heart to know that there are thousands of unwanted children with Down syndrome—certainly, the children are missing out and hurting. But the moms, dads, brothers, sisters, cousins, neighbors, friends....they are the ones truly missing out.

Stephen and Lila have old Scooby Doo figures that they play with together constantly. The figures are broken and missing parts—Shaggy is missing arms, legs, and his head, Scooby's eyes and ears have fallen out, Daphne is just a head, Velma's paint is chipped and flaking off. To Stephen and Lila, these imperfections don't matter. They play with them the same as they would play with brand new, complete action figures. I love this picture of their acceptance and love. I hope and pray that the rest of the world learns to emulate this attitude—only with people, not action figures.

The Love of Georgie

Written by: Archbishop Joseph Kurtz

"You're the big brother. You will have to look after Joe." My sisters spoke, pretending to be serious, and exchanging playful glances with each other and me.

On this good advice, my brother George, who is 48 years old and has Down Syndrome, came to live with me at St. Mary's Rectory in Catasauqua, Pa. Little did we realize how true these words would become.

At the rectory, Georgie has contributed in countless ways. He is a community builder par excellence. Two weeks had not gone by before he had given each person on the rectory staff a nickname. In the Old Testament, God gave Abram a new name to claim him as his own, and so Georgie quickly claimed us as part of his family.

Through a playful "boo," an occasional hug, and a pat on the back, Georgie brought to the rectory an ease that became infectious. He became a co-worker. Recently, when he announced that he would be going for a week's vacation with one of his sisters, everyone was up in arms at what they would do while he was gone.

He is a friend in the evening. I now know the TV schedule for most evenings after 9:30 p.m. (I have not had a schedule down this well since eighth grade.) This has been a time to stop and pause and enjoy. From the very beginning, Georgie knew what we have just slowly discovered in four months — that he is looking after me and so many others.

Recently, after celebrating a Mass for our dear mother, I must have looked a little down to him. He gave me a pat on the back and said, "Don't worry. Mom is in heaven. You have me." Giving and receiving are intertwined. We never do one exclusively. In the case of my relating to my brother, it is not a cliché to say I have received much more than I have given.

That's the nature of Christian community. The love of Christ calls all of us to be good givers and good receivers and so to love.

Growing up with Angel

Written by: DeAnna Pursai

Growing up with Angel always at my side was an exhilarating and amazing ride! Angel was always so full of joy, energy, laughter, enthusiasm. I was mostly always known as, "Angel's big sister – and I loved it!" Everybody in our small hometown of Bluffton, Indiana knew Angel – as well as folks from surrounding counties around.

I remember when I was about 5 years old Angel had to go to Indianapolis for a long time to Riley Children's Hospital to have open heart surgery. I don't remember a lot, but I remember lots of crying and fear and loneliness. My grandmother came to stay with me, and it was so strange not having her around. I was so relieved when she came back home and things settled down to our normal, crazy house again full of energy, laughter, joy, exuberance.

Angel was a ball of energy growing up. On Friday nights when we all sat around watching JR Ewing on the Dallas tv show, Angel loved to tie a towel around her neck like she had a cape, stand at the end of one room, and insist that we "announce" her performance, and then proceed to go to the center of the living room and entertain us with dancing and singing her every commercial.

We had a lakehouse in northern Indiana called Lake Wawasee. We spent hundreds of hours up there hanging out, eating hot dogs, playing in the lake, having fun. My dad even named our boat after her, calling it "Angel II." She loved to take the wheel of the boat when we were out in the lake. We spent many birthday parties out in the middle of the lake in our boat with the anchor down. I can remember fondly Angel pretending to be fishing at the end of our Pier. She could stay out there for hours pretending to be fishing. Another fun pastime Angel liked to do was sit down on the end of the pier and wave to the people in the boats with her foot! She'd take off her shoes and socks and wave at everyone bare-footed!

I remember once Angel ran out into the middle of the cornfield near our barn one late afternoon, and my mom couldn't find her. I think half the town was out there looking for her in that field. It was getting dark, and I remember distinctly my mom crying. Then out she ran from one of the aisles of corn all covered with dirt. She  was certainly a kid on the go! Another time I'll never forget is our school bus rides with our favorite bus driver, Ralph Schwartz. Angel could never say "Ralph" – so she called him "Rife." To this day, we tease her about calling him "Rife." One day when we got on the bus after I had been sick the previous day, Ralph said to me, "Are you feeling better." Angel announced to everyone on the bus, "She had diarrhea." I could have strangled her I was so embarrassed.

Angel taught me so very much how to be fun, care-free, loving, kind, and patient. She always had a nice word to say about everyone, well – most people. One time when my dad had just gotten email, and she loved to check it, one of his friends had sent him a dirty joke. Angel saw it before my dad, and she never forgave him for that. She is strong, independent and loves to make people happy. I love my sister, Angel, with all of my heart and soul, and I am most definitely a better person because of the wonderful life lessons she teaches me each time I am around her. I love you, Angelletti Michetti!

Acknowledgements

I want to take a few moments to thank all the people who helped make this book possible. A BIG thank you from me goes out to all of you siblings who shared your story in this book! My hope and prayer is that the stories in this book, will reach out to those parents who just found out their baby has Down syndrome - and that from reading that their baby with Down syndrome will be a blessing to their sibling - they will choose LIFE.

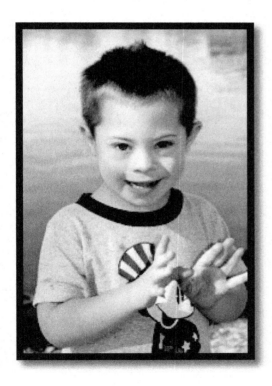

Also I have a lot of family members I want to thank. Mom and Dad, thank you, thank you, thank you, thank you!!! You've kept me on track and encouraged me to keep going. You also helped cultivate a passion for wanting to protect life and care for the widows and orphans.

There are so many others that I wanted to thank for helping me make this book a reality. Mr. Carleton, thank you so much for creating the beautiful book cover. Mr. Zink, thank you for helping with the legal side of things. A big thank you also goes out to all of the friends and family who have promoted Beauty

Exposed, encouraged me, and given me the passion to keep going!!!

Last, but not by any means least, I want to thank God for giving me the passion for life and for wanting to protect. HE is the reason that there is a book called Beauty Exposed; HE is the reason I have two BEAUTIFUL siblings with Down syndrome and HE is the reason that I am alive!

About the Author

Chloe Goulding lives in San Jose, California with her two sisters (Ellie & Charity), three brothers (Tucker, Harrison & Neko), and mom and dad. In her free time Chloe enjoys reading Nancy Drew, doing worship dance, baking treats in the kitchen, and spending time together with her family! She loves volunteering and helping out with kids who have special needs /adopted/in foster care.

If this book impacted you, she would love to hear from you ~ you can email her at; chloe@beautyexposedthebook.com

Epilogue

I am so happy that you've had the chance to read through these stories written by people who all have something in common - a sibling with Down syndrome. This book you are holding has been in the making about 2 years now.

I am now 17 years old, and just starting college (early - I know!). I am still planning on being a nurse, and am looking into which college would be the best to attend for a nursing degree. I recently volunteered for a week at a Joni and Friends Family Retreat near my house, and can't wait to volunteer again in the years to come!

The idea for Beauty Exposed came to me probably a year before I actually started collecting stories. I had read the first "Gifts" book edited by Kathryn Lynard Soper. This book includes stories all written by mothers who have a child with Down

syndrome. Their stories share what they felt and how they dealt with the diagnosis of Down syndrome. After reading it, I mentioned how neat it would be if there was a book just like that, but from the siblings' perspectives. My parents told me that I should be the one to publish a book from siblings perspectives...and time went by, with the idea still in the back of my head, and I knew I needed to do it!

Writing is not my favorite thing to do, and I had no idea how to publish a book, so those two things combined made for a very interesting adventure. I knew I needed to put this book together because I believe strongly that every human being, born or unborn, has the right to life. Those of us who love someone with Down syndrome have a duty to speak up for our siblings, friends and family; to give them a voice and show the world that all people have worth and deserve our respect.

In the many stories I've read about giving birth to a child with Down syndrome, there is almost always a similar question asked by the parents: "How will this child with a "disability" affect the children that I already have?" I want this book to show parents that this child with Down syndrome will be like any other sibling, and that they don't need to be afraid for the children they already have. I also want this book to be an encouragement to the siblings of someone with Down syndrome. We are all in this together, as we live with these amazing people, loving them with all our hearts!

CPSIA information can be obtained
at www.ICGtesting.com
Printed in the USA
BVOW06s0139311016

466480BV00005B/56/P